A FAMILY COOKBOOK

Makan *at* Mum's

Jeanie Lau & Katrina Lau Hammond

Bernard, Jeanie & friend Fung hometown Ipoh 1963

New Years Eve Street Party hosts, Girraang 1976

Jeanie's mother's 70th birthday celebration, Sydney 1996

Colin's 9th birthday with Jeanie's parents and family

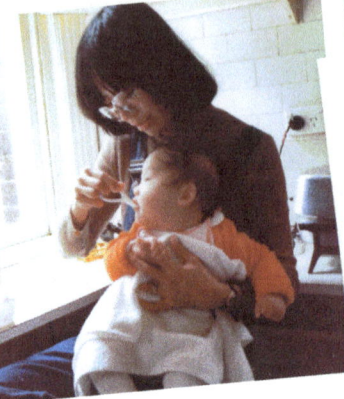
Breakfast time, Colin and Jeanie, Birchgrove 1979

Jeanie and Eddie on their honeymoon in Hong Kong, 1976

Katrina at 15 months, raiding the pantry

Colin, 1 year old, having a go with chopsticks

Banquet spread for Colin's 1 month old party (Moon Yuet)

Chinese New Year gathering with neighbours in Canberra 1977-78

The family at a chinese restaurant, 1986

Jeanie showing Justin how to bake a chiffon for his uncle's birthday, 2021

Hosting a steamboat dinner party for work colleagues, 1970's

Enjoying Indian curry in Singapore, 2019

Behind the scenes for our recipe book, 2020

Colin's 3rd birthday clown cake with Amy and Danny

Katrina's 4th birthday with Ffrosty, Nanna, Jeanie's father

Eddie at Chinese New Year feast 2021

Food markets while on holidays 2015

Jeanie's birthday buns and egg tarts with family and friends, 1984

Decorating a pavlova together

Two birthday cakes for their mum, Katrina's birthday, 2021

Fathers Day Picnic, 2020

Cupcakes by Justin, 2020

Colin's birthday 2021

Katrina, Jeanie and Eddie's mother, Boxing Day 2004

Jeanie and Eddie with the mud crab, Lake Macquarie

Jeanie and Eddie teaching their grandkids how to make wontons, 2018

Cupcakes by Mackenzie, 2020

Acknowledgments

*The authors would like to sincerely thank all
those that have been involved in the development,
funding, production and promotion of this book.
We couldn't have done it without your support.*

*To all you kind-hearted people who believed
in our project and backed it, financially
and emotionally, we thank you.*

Now, makan! (Let's eat!)

To Justin and Mackenzie, be adventurous.
To my family, sweet memories of good times.
—J.

For Jeanie – our Mum and Por Por
– to mark seven wonderful decades.
Thank you for sharing your love of food, your
passion for cooking, and for nourishing us.
– K.

Contents

Appetisers *and* Salads | **11**

Light Meals | **39**

Rice *and* Noodles | **53**

Shared Dishes | **83**

Desserts *and* Cakes | **129**

Basics | **166**

Sauces Pantry | **168**

Dry Pantry | **171**

Index | **172**

ne of our dear friends translated the Chinese saying 食得是福 as "it is a blessing that there is food and you can eat what you like and as much as you like". Although we are currently living under the restrictions brought about by COVID19, we are fortunate indeed to live in Australia and despite our ethnic diversity we are one and free. Living in the 50s, I can remember the only outside food we enjoyed eating were meat pies and fish and chips. Now, you only have to look at establishments offering food delivery to choose the different types of food that are available. Whilst my wife, Jeanie, said modestly that her dishes are home cooking, they are cooked with love and passion for the family to enjoy. We hope that this cookbook with its numerous recipes on appetisers, mains, desserts as well as cakes will provide the inspiration and incentives to cook for your family. I would like to take this opportunity to congratulate the Fabulous 4: my wife, Jeanie, daughter, Katrina, daughter-in-law, Mei and son, Colin, for their tireless work during the last 12 months in bringing this project to fruition. In conclusion, I would like to use the saying in Chinese banquets 飲飽食醉 "drink until full and eat until drunk".

Eddie Lau
June 2021

Appetisers *and* Salads

Spring Rolls

MAKES 20–25 PIECES

1 packet 20 cm (8") square spring roll wrappers (20–25 pieces)

1 egg, lightly beaten, for sealing the rolls

Oil, for frying

2 Tbsp oil

1 clove garlic, minced

400 g (14 oz) minced pork, or turkey, or chicken

¼ white cabbage, finely chopped (about 3 cups)

2 carrots, peeled and shredded (about 2 cups)

1 small tin (227 g, 8 oz) water chestnuts, chopped

1 Tbsp oyster sauce, or 1 tsp chicken stock powder

1 tsp salt

2 tsp soy sauce

1 tsp cornflour (cornstarch) (+ 1 tsp extra)

1 In a non-stick frypan over medium heat, add the oil and garlic and fry until slightly golden. Add the mince, breaking up the lumps and turning the meat until it changes colour.

2 Add the cabbage and carrots and cook until the cabbage starts to wilt. Add the water chestnuts. Then add in the seasoning (oyster sauce or chicken powder, salt, soy sauce). Cook, stirring until the liquid has evaporated. Turn off the heat and sprinkle 1 tsp cornflour over the filling and mix it in. The filling should not be watery. Add another teaspoon of cornflour if necessary. Cool the filling before making the spring rolls.

3 Peel apart the spring roll wrappers. Cover with a tea towel.

4 Place a wrapper, smooth side down, in a diamond position. Spoon 1 tablespoon of filling on the wrapper about 10 cm (4") from the bottom, leaving 5 cm (2") on both sides. Take the bottom corner and tuck it snugly over the filling. Fold the two sides in and roll up to the top, using the beaten egg to seal the last corner of the wrapper. Give it a roll back and forth gently. Repeat until all the filling is used up.

5 Fill a saucepan with frying oil to about the halfway mark. Heat on medium-high. Test with a wooden chopstick. If rapid bubbles appear around it, it's hot enough. The oil must not be too hot.

6 Fry 5–6 spring rolls at a time, until the rolls are golden brown on both sides. Remove and drain off the oil. Transfer the rolls onto paper towels. Repeat until all the rolls are cooked. Serve with sweet and sour sauce (see recipe below).

Sweet & Sour Sauce

½ cup (125 mL) rice vinegar

⅓ cup (75 g) sugar

2 Tbsp tomato sauce (ketchup)

2 tsp soy sauce

2½ tsp cornflour (cornstarch)

2 Tbsp water

1 Combine the first 4 ingredients in a small saucepan over medium heat.

2 Bring to a boil, then lower heat. Mix the cornflour and water together. Stir into the simmering sauce to thicken.

Curry Puffs

A good finger food for entertaining, or as a snack during the day.

MAKES 16

5 Tbsp oil

1 medium onion, finely diced

2 tsp chicken curry powder (e.g. Clive of India brand)

½ tsp chilli powder (optional)

300 g (10½ oz) chicken mince

3 large potatoes, boiled or steamed, diced

½ tsp salt

½ tsp black pepper

Handful of coriander (cilantro) or parsley, finely chopped (optional)

4 sheets ready-rolled puff pastry, or shortcrust pastry

1 egg, lightly beaten

1 Heat the oil in a wok. Fry the onions until golden brown. Add in the curry powder and chilli powder and fry gently. Put in the chicken mince and stir-fry. Then add in the potatoes, salt and black pepper. Cook for 5 mins, adding a bit of water if it's too dry. Mix well and leave to cool. Sprinkle the coriander or parsley over the filling.

2 Cut the ready-made pastry into 8 cm (3") circles (in diameter). Put 1 Tbsp of meat filling in the middle. Fold the pastry over to make a semicircle and press the edges together. Using your thumb and index finger, indent the edge and roll to crimp. Repeat until the half circle is done. Repeat until all the filling is used up.

3 Place the curry puffs on a lined baking tray. Brush beaten egg over the curry puffs.

4 Bake in a preheated 180°C (360°F) oven until golden brown, approx. 25 mins.

....

Variation:

Follow steps 1 and 2, then heat some frying oil in a saucepan until hot. Deep fry the curry puffs in batches until golden. Remove and drain on paper towel.

War Tip ~ Pan Fried Pork Dumplings

There are many different versions of fillings for 'war tip', also known as 'pot stickers'. This is generally what I put in. Feel free to change the recipe or substitute what you like.

MAKES 30 PIECES

160 g (5½ oz) white cabbage, or wombok (Chinese cabbage)
200 g (7 oz) pork mince
1 Tbsp soy sauce
1 Tbsp oyster sauce
2 tsp oil
1 tsp sesame oil
Dash of pepper
½ tsp salt
½ tsp sugar
1 tsp chicken stock powder
1½ Tbsp cornflour (cornstarch)
1 packet gow gee wrappers* (30 pieces)
Oil, for frying
Water, for sealing and steaming

1 Wash the cabbage, drain, and chop finely.

2 Mix the minced pork with the sauces, oils, pepper, salt, sugar, chicken powder and cornflour. Add in the chopped cabbage and mix well. Place the meat mixture in the fridge if not using straight away.

3 Put 2 teaspoons of filling in the middle of the wrapper. Wet the edge of the wrapper with water. Fold in half and make 4–5 pleats on one side and press to the flat side to seal. Or you can just press both edges together and seal. Repeat with the remaining meat mixture.

4 Heat 1 Tbsp oil in a frypan. Line up the dumplings in the pan and cook for 2 mins to brown lightly, then add water to come halfway up the dumplings. Cover with a lid and cook (steam) for 10 mins.

5 When all the water has evaporated, add a little oil around the pan. Fry on low heat until the bottoms of the dumplings are golden brown. Turn off heat, stand for 1–2 mins. Turn the dumplings over onto a plate with the browned bottoms facing up.

6 Repeat with the remaining dumplings. Serve with dumpling sauce (see recipe below).

Dumpling Sauce

1 Tbsp black vinegar (chin kiang vinegar)
1 Tbsp light soy sauce
2 tsp sugar
1 tsp finely shredded or minced ginger

Mix ingredients together and serve with dumplings.

*Gow gee wrappers are round and white. Sometimes called gyoza wrappers.

Acar Awak ~ Malaysian Pickled Vegetables

SERVES 4

Pickled Cucumber
400 g (14 oz) continental cucumber
3 tsp salt
1 Tbsp sugar
3 Tbsp white vinegar

Scalded Vegetables
600 mL (20 fl oz) water
400 mL (13½ fl oz) vinegar
1 Tbsp salt
1 Tbsp sugar
100 g (3½ oz) carrots, cut into strips 3 cm long x 3 mm wide (1¼" x ⅛")
100 g (3½ oz) green beans or snake beans, cut into 3 cm lengths (1¼")
100 g (3½ oz) cauliflower, cut into small florets
300 g (10½ oz) cabbage, cut into pieces 5 cm long x 3 cm wide (2" x 1¼")

Spice Paste
5 cloves garlic, sliced
1 medium red onion, chopped
1 x 2.5 cm (1") piece fresh galangal, sliced
1 x 2.5 cm (1") piece fresh turmeric, sliced
1 stalk lemongrass, white part only, chopped
5 long red chillies, chopped (use more if preferred)

½ cup vegetable oil
2 Tbsp sugar
4 Tbsp vinegar
1–2 tsp salt
100 g (3½ oz) fresh pineapple, cut into small pieces

100 g (3½ oz) roasted peanuts*, roughly chopped, to serve
1 Tbsp toasted sesame seeds˄, to serve

A spicy and sour pickle, you can substitute other vegetables, such as okra or eggplant.

1 To pickle the cucumber, quarter the cucumber lengthwise, skin on. Remove the seeds, cut into 3 cm (1¼") long strips. Put the cucumbers together with the salt, sugar and white vinegar and pickle for 1 hour. After an hour, squeeze out as much liquid from the cucumbers as you can. Set aside.

2 Scald the vegetables separately. Put the water, vinegar, salt and sugar in a large saucepan over high heat. Blanch the carrots, green beans or snake beans and cauliflower florets for 1 min. Remove and drain in a colander. Blanch the cabbage for 30 secs. Drain.

3 Blend the spice paste ingredients together in a food processor.

4 Heat the oil in a wok over medium-high heat. Fry the blended spice paste for 5 mins until aromatic and dark brown in colour. Lower the heat. Season with sugar, vinegar and salt. Cook for a few minutes. Taste and adjust the balance. Spice paste should have thickened. Mix well. Turn off heat. Leave to cool.

5 Add the pickled cucumber, scalded vegetables and pineapple pieces into the spice paste and stir well to coat. Transfer to a glass container. Leave in the fridge overnight for the flavours to develop.

6 To serve, scoop the acar onto a serving dish. Sprinkle with chopped peanuts and toasted sesame seeds.

Note: Acar can keep for two weeks in the fridge. Do not add the peanuts if not serving straight away.

*See 'Basics' on page 167 for how to roast peanuts.
˄To toast sesame seeds: dry fry the seeds in a frypan over low heat until lightly toasted.

Malaysian Chicken Satay

MAKES 12–15 SKEWERS

500 g (1 lb 2 oz) chicken thigh fillets
1 stalk lemongrass, white part only, cut into small rounds
1 clove garlic, peeled
¼ brown onion, chopped
1 tsp turmeric powder
1 tsp cumin powder
2 tsp coriander powder
1 tsp chilli powder (optional)
2 Tbsp oil
1 tsp salt
1 Tbsp sugar

15 bamboo skewers
½ red onion, cut into small chunks
1 cucumber, cut into small chunks

Spice Mix

3 cloves garlic, peeled
4 small shallots (eschalots), or ¼ onion
1 stalk lemongrass
1 tsp galangal powder
1 tsp chilli powder (optional)
1 tsp coriander powder

¼ cup (60 mL) oil
1 cup (155 g) dry roasted peanuts*, crushed
1½ Tbsp wet tamarind puree (e.g. Golden Choice brand)
1 cup (250 mL) water
2 tsp salt
2½ Tbsp sugar
2 tsp vinegar

1 Cut the chicken into 2.5 cm x 4 cm (1" x 1½") pieces and set aside.

2 Pound or blend the lemongrass, garlic and onion until fine. Add the turmeric, cumin, coriander and chilli powders, oil, salt and sugar.

3 Combine the chicken and the spice mixture. Mix well and leave to marinate for at least 1 hour, or refrigerate overnight.

4 While marinating, or the next day, soak the bamboo skewers in water.

5 Thread 3–4 pieces of chicken onto one end of the skewers.

6 Grill the chicken for 2–3 mins each side or until cooked, basting with a bit of oil while cooking.

7 Serve the chicken satay hot with cut red onion and cucumber on the side, with a bowl of satay sauce (see recipe below) and some acar awak (optional, see recipe on previous page).

Tip: For small amounts, you can use a microplane to grate the lemongrass, garlic and onion into a bowl. Just be careful not to cut your fingers.

Satay Sauce

1 For the spice mix, pound the garlic, shallots and white part of the lemongrass till fine in a mortar and pestle, or blend in a food processor. Add in the galangal, chilli and coriander powders. Mix well.

2 In a small saucepan, heat the oil on medium-low heat. Add the spice mixture in and the remaining top section of the lemongrass. Fry until aromatic.

3 Add in the peanuts, tamarind puree, water, salt, sugar and vinegar. Stir the mixture until well incorporated. Cook the sauce on medium-low heat for 5–10 mins until the sauce thickens to the desired consistency, and the oil separates out. Taste and adjust seasoning. Discard the lemongrass pieces before spooning into a sauce bowl.

4 Cool. Serve with satay chicken.

Tip: Refrigerate any leftover sauce. When reheating, if the sauce is too thick, dilute with a bit of water or vinegar.

*See 'Basics' on page 167 for how to roast peanuts.

Facing page features pottery side dishes, hand-made by Jeanie (1980s)

In Malaysia, satay is a common street-food, popular with both kids and adults. Back in the 1980s in Sydney, our family had a satay shop in the city called "Just Satay", selling skewers of chicken, pork, beef and prawn satay.

Thai Fish Cakes

SERVES 4

500 g (1 lb 2 oz) fish fillets e.g. ling, perch, hoki

3 Tbsp red curry paste (e.g. Maesri brand)

50 mL (1¾ fl oz) fish sauce

1 egg, lightly beaten

1 tsp caster sugar (superfine sugar)

60 mL (2 fl oz) water

2 Tbsp cornflour (cornstarch)

8–10 green beans, or 4 snake beans (long beans), finely cut

8–10 kaffir lime leaves*, finely sliced

Vegetable oil, for frying

Sweet chilli sauce, to serve

1 Cut the fish into chunks.

2 Place the fish, curry paste, fish sauce, egg, sugar and water in a food processor and blend until the fish is finely minced.

3 Transfer the fish paste to a large mixing bowl.

4 Mix in the cornflour, beans and lime leaves until they are well combined. Gather the fish into a ball and pound it against the bowl a few times until the texture is springy / bouncy.

5 Mould the fish paste into small (30–32 g / 1 oz) patties about 1 cm (⅜") thick.

6 Pour some oil in a small frypan up to about 2.5 cm (1") deep. Heat up the oil. Shallow fry the fish cakes until golden brown, about 2–3 mins. Flip over and brown the other side. Remove and place on a dish with paper towel to drain. Repeat with the rest of the fish mixture. Add more oil to the pan if needed.

7 Serve fish cakes while hot, with sweet chilli sauce.

*Remove main rib of lime leaves. Roll up into a cigar and slice finely. Lime leaves can be substituted with coriander (cilantro) leaves and young stems.

Suen Laht Tong ~ Hot *and* Sour Soup

This soup is popular in Peking restaurants. The heat comes from the white pepper and the chilli oil, so adjust to your liking.

SERVES 4–6

100 g (3½ oz) chicken or pork meat, thinly sliced into strips

1 tsp soy sauce

1 tsp oil

1 tsp cornflour (cornstarch)

1 Tbsp water

4 cups (1 litre) chicken stock*

6 dried shiitake mushrooms, soaked till soft, thinly sliced

¼ cup (50 g) bamboo shoot strips

¼ cup dried black wood fungus^ (mook yee), soaked to soften, thinly sliced

½ tsp ginger, grated

¼ cup (60 mL) soy sauce

⅓ cup (80 mL) rice vinegar, or white vinegar

⅓ cup cornflour (cornstarch)

¼ cup (60 mL) water

200 g (7 oz) firm tofu, cut into 1.3 cm (½") cubes or strips

2 eggs, lightly beaten

½ tsp salt

White pepper, to taste

2 green shallots (green onions / scallions), chopped

½ tsp sesame oil

½ tsp chilli oil, or dried chilli flakes (optional)

1 Marinate the chicken or pork with the soy sauce, oil, cornflour and water. Set aside.

2 Bring the chicken stock to the boil in a large stock pot. Add the mushrooms, bamboo shoots, wood fungus, ginger, soy sauce and rice vinegar and stir to combine. Cook over medium heat for 5–10 mins.

3 Add the marinated chicken or pork to the soup. Cook for 1 min.

4 Mix ⅓ cup cornflour and ¼ cup water into a slurry paste. Once the soup has reached a simmer, stir the cornflour mixture into the soup to thicken.

5 Add in the tofu. Continue stirring the soup in a circular motion while drizzling the beaten eggs in a thin stream to create ribbons. Season to taste with salt and white pepper.

6 Stir in the green shallots and sesame oil. Drizzle with chilli oil or sprinkle with chilli flakes to serve, if desired.

Notes:

A) If you like a more sour soup, add in more vinegar.

B) Add extra white pepper for a more fragrant, spicy taste.

C) Add some lai mein (wheat noodles) to this soup for a complete meal.

*See 'Basics' on page 167 for how to make homemade chicken stock.

^Black wood fungus (mook yee) is larger, thicker and crunchier than cloud ear fungus (wan yee).

Sang Choy Bao

Often served in Chinese restaurants as an entrée (starter), this recipe is family-friendly and easy to make at home.

MAKES 12

1½ Tbsp oil

1 tsp ginger, minced

2 cloves garlic, minced

1 small onion, chopped

500 g (1 lb 2 oz) pork mince

2 larp cheong (Chinese sausages), finely chopped

1 medium carrot, finely chopped

200 g (7 oz) water chestnuts, chopped

10 green beans, finely diced

2 tsp cornflour (cornstarch), mixed with 4 Tbsp water

1 green shallot (green onion / scallion), chopped, for garnish (optional)

12 iceberg lettuce leaves, or butter lettuce leaves*

Sauce

2 Tbsp light soy sauce

1½ tsp dark soy sauce

2 Tbsp oyster sauce

1 tsp sugar

1 Mix the sauce ingredients together in a small bowl.

2 Heat the oil in a wok over medium-high heat. Add the ginger, garlic and onion and stir-fry for 1–2 mins.

3 Add the pork mince, cook, stirring and breaking up the lumps until the pork changes colour. Then add the larp cheong and mix it in with the pork.

4 Add the carrot, water chestnuts and green beans. Cook for 2 mins, stirring and tossing to mix them in.

5 Add the sauce in and stir-fry quickly. Stir in half the cornflour mixture to thicken the sauce. If the sauce is still watery, thicken further with the remaining cornflour mixture.

6 Transfer the meat filling into a serving dish. Sprinkle with green shallots, if desired.

7 To serve, spoon some filling onto a lettuce leaf. Enclose the filling and eat with your fingers.

*Trim the iceberg lettuce leaf into a round bowl shape with scissors. Butter lettuce, coral lettuce or baby cos (little gem) lettuce leaves could be used whole.

New Year Yu Sang ~ Prosperity Toss Salad

SERVES 6–8

Fish
300 g (10½ oz) smoked salmon, or 500 g (1 lb 2 oz) sashimi-grade raw salmon

Salad
6–8 iceberg lettuce leaves, shredded

2 medium carrots, julienned

½ daikon (white radish), julienned

2 Lebanese cucumbers, julienned (liquid squeezed out)

1 small packet Japanese pickled ginger

1 pomelo or ruby red grapefruit, cut into small pieces

1 bottle of Chinese mixed pickles, cut into strips (e.g. Mee Chun HK brand)

Condiments / Garnishes
10 wonton wrappers (egg pastry skins)

1 packet peanut candy, crushed

2 Tbsp sesame seeds, toasted*

4–5 Tbsp caster sugar (superfine sugar)

2 green shallots (green onions / scallions), finely sliced

2–3 stalks coriander (cilantro), roughly chopped

6 kaffir lime leaves, finely sliced^

Dressing
4 Tbsp extra virgin olive oil, or garlic oil

1 Tbsp sesame oil

2–3 Tbsp brandy (optional)

½ cup white vinegar, or rice vinegar, or apple cider vinegar

2 tsp salt

½ tsp pepper

1 If using sashimi raw salmon instead of smoked salmon, slice the raw salmon and place on a plate. Wrap and chill in the fridge.

2 Cut the wonton wrappers into 1.3 cm (½") squares and deep fry until golden brown and crispy. Drain on paper towel and set aside.

3 Prep the salad items and refrigerate in containers.

4 Prep the condiments / garnishes and put them each in separate bowls.

5 An hour before serving, arrange the salad items in groups on a large round platter. Place the salmon slices (smoked or raw) in the centre on top of the salad and surround it with the crispy wonton strips, peanut candy and sesame seeds.

6 Sprinkle the sugar, green shallots, coriander leaves and lime leaves over the salad.

7 Spoon over the olive oil, sesame oil, brandy and vinegar. Season with salt and pepper.

8 Diners then toss and mix the salad with their chopsticks. In the New Year they say 'loh hei' meaning 'rise and prosper'. Then they place some salad on their plate with some sashimi or smoked salmon.

Note: You could provide the components of the dressing so diners can adjust the seasoning to their liking.

*To toast sesame seeds: dry fry the seeds in a frypan over low heat until lightly toasted.

^Remove main rib of lime leaves, roll into a cigar and slice finely.

Traditionally, this symbolic Malaysian-Chinese dish, also known as 'loh sang', is served on the 7th day ('Yan Yet'—Everybody's Birthday) of the lunar new year. But over time it has become popular to serve it on Chinese New Year's Day. Serve at lunch with chicken congee or noodles, or as first course (usually) at a dinner banquet.

Tom Yum Goong
~ Thai Hot *and* Sour Soup *with* Prawns

SERVES 2

3 cups chicken stock*, or water

12 fresh prawns, peeled and deveined (reserve heads and shells for stock)

3 cloves garlic, crushed

3 green shallots (green onions / scallions), white part only, sliced into 2.5 cm (1") pieces

1 stalk lemongrass, white part only, sliced diagonally

5 slices ginger

100 g (3½ oz) mushrooms, cut in half e.g. button, straw, oyster

1 tomato, cut into 8 pieces

Fresh chillies, sliced

2 Tbsp fish sauce

4 kaffir lime leaves, torn roughly

1½ Tbsp lime juice

2 stalks coriander (cilantro), chopped

1 Bring the stock or water to the boil. Put in the prawn peelings and boil for 10 mins. Remove and discard the prawn peelings.

2 Add in the garlic, white parts of the shallots, lemongrass and ginger and boil for 5 mins. Then add the mushrooms and tomatoes and bring back to the boil. Add the chillies, fish sauce and lime leaves. Cook for 5 mins, then add the prawns and cook for about 1–2 mins. Stir in the lime juice. Turn off the heat.

3 Adjust to taste, adding more chilli, fish sauce or lime juice as needed. Serve garnished with coriander.

Note: Soup could be served with noodles or rice, if desired.

*See 'Basics' on page 167 for how to make homemade chicken stock.

Larb Woon Sen ~ Thai Spicy Pork Bean Thread Noodle Salad

A "salad" that is served warm. Deliciously spiced mince tossed through clear noodles, you can adjust the spiciness, saltiness and sourness to your liking.

SERVES 4

- 1½ Tbsp glutinous rice, toasted
- 1 packet (100 g, 3½ oz) bean thread vermicelli, soaked
- ½ cup (125 mL) water
- 1 tsp chicken stock powder
- 200 g (7 oz) pork mince, or chicken mince
- 15 g (½ oz) dried shrimps, soaked
- 1 clove garlic, minced
- 1–1½ Tbsp chilli paste with soybean oil (e.g. Pantai brand)
- 1 Tbsp fish sauce
- 2 lemons, juiced
- 1 red onion, thinly sliced
- 4 Tbsp coriander (cilantro) leaves, chopped
- 4 kaffir lime leaves, very finely sliced^
- 1 fresh red chilli, sliced, or chilli flakes, to serve (optional)
- Extra coriander (cilantro), to serve
- 1 lemon, cut into wedges, to serve

1. Pound the toasted rice in a mortar and pestle. Set aside.

2. Drain the bean thread vermicelli and cut into shorter lengths. Steep in hot water for 1–2 mins to soften. Drain and set aside.

3. Put ½ cup water and the chicken powder in a frypan over medium heat. Add in the pork mince, shrimps and garlic and cook until the meat changes colour. Lower the heat, add the chilli paste, fish sauce and lemon juice. Then add the vermicelli and gently mix in with tongs or chopsticks. Turn off the heat.

4. Mix in the sliced onion, coriander and lime leaves. Taste and adjust with lemon juice.

5. Dish up, sprinkle the toasted rice on top and garnish with the chillies, coriander and lemon wedges.

6. Serve as a shared side or main dish.

^Remove main rib of lime leaves, roll into a cigar and slice very finely.

Thai Beef Salad

*A refreshing, light salad dish that goes well with grilled prawns or squid too.
Taste and adjust the dressing, balancing out the sweet, salty, sour and spicy flavours.*

SERVES 4

250 g (8¾ oz) beef sirloin
1 Tbsp oil
Salt and pepper
2 cups mixed lettuce leaves
8 cherry tomatoes, halved
¼ small red onion, finely sliced
¼ cup mint leaves
¼ cup coriander (cilantro) leaves, lightly packed
Extra mint leaves, for garnish
Extra coriander leaves, for garnish

Dressing

3 kaffir lime leaves
2–3 coriander (cilantro) roots and stems
2 cloves garlic, peeled
1 small chilli / birds eye chilli, chopped
2 Tbsp sugar
2 Tbsp fish sauce
3 Tbsp lime juice

1 For the dressing, remove the main rib of the lime leaves, roll into a cigar and slice finely. Dice the coriander stems.

2 Pound the garlic, chilli and coriander roots in a mortar and pestle until fine.

3 Add the sugar, fish sauce and lime juice to the mortar. Mix in. Adjust to taste. Add in the finely sliced lime leaves and the diced coriander stems. Set aside.

4 Preheat a frypan or skillet until hot. Drizzle the beef with ½ Tbsp oil on both sides. Season with salt and pepper. Cook the beef for 2–3 mins each side, or to your liking. Rest the meat.

Assemble salad:

5 Place some lettuce leaves in a mixing bowl. Drizzle with 1 Tbsp dressing and toss gently with your fingers.

6 Slice the beef thinly. Place beef in a separate bowl with the remaining salad ingredients — lettuce, tomatoes, onions, mint and coriander. Toss gently with some of the remaining dressing.

7 Place the dressed lettuce onto a plate. Pile the beef and other salad ingredients on top. Garnish with the extra mint and coriander. Drizzle over any remaining dressing. Serve immediately.

Som Tum ~ Green Papaya Salad

A light, healthy salad allowing the main components — green papaya, beans, tomatoes and peanuts — to shine. Normally served as an entrée (starter) but would go very well with Thai fried rice, or as a meal. This salad pairs well with seafood.

SERVES 4

400 g (14 oz) green papaya, peeled, deseeded and shredded

3 snake beans (long beans), cut into 5 cm (2") lengths

8 cherry tomatoes, halved

40 g (1⅜ oz) peanuts, roasted,* roughly chopped

Dressing

1 clove garlic, peeled

2 fresh red chillies

2 tsp (4 g) dried shrimps, soaked in hot water 10 mins, drained

2 Tbsp lime juice

2 Tbsp fish sauce

1 Tbsp palm sugar, grated, or caster sugar (superfine sugar)

1 For the dressing, pound the garlic and chillies in a deep mortar and pestle until crushed, then add the dried shrimps and pound until softened.

2 Add the lime juice, fish sauce and palm sugar to the mortar and stir with the pestle or a spoon until dissolved.

3 Add the papaya, beans and tomatoes to the mortar and pound gently with the pestle to bruise and soften the vegetables.

4 Adjust seasoning to taste — balancing sweet, sour, spicy and salty. Finally, add the roasted peanuts and mix well.

5 Dish up. Salad could be served with grilled prawns (as pictured), fish cake, squid, or on its own.

 To make it a vegetarian dish, simply take out the shrimps and fish sauce. Add a bit of salt or soy sauce back to replace the fish sauce.

*See 'Basics' on page 167 for how to roast peanuts.

Light Meals

Siu Mai ~ Chinese Steamed Dumplings

A "must have" menu item at yum cha or dim sum restaurants, that you can now make at home. Make a big batch and freeze them.

MAKES 30 PIECES

400 g (14 oz) pork mince with some fat (not too lean)

4 dried shiitake mushrooms, soaked, finely diced

250 g (8¾ oz) raw prawns, cut into ½ cm (¼") pieces (optional)

1 packet egg pastry skins / wonton wrappers (e.g. Double Merino brand)

1 green shallot (green onion / scallion), white part sliced into small rounds (optional)

Chilli sauce, to serve (optional)

Seasoning

1½ tsp salt

4 tsp sugar

¼ tsp pepper

1 tsp sesame oil

2½ tsp rice wine

1½ Tbsp cornflour (cornstarch)

1 egg white

50 mL (1¾ fl oz) water

1 Mix the seasoning ingredients together in a mixing bowl. Add the pork mince in and mix vigorously until the mixture is pasty. Add the mushrooms, prawns (if using) and mix in well.

2 Using a butter knife, put some filling in the centre of the pastry wrapper. Shape the dumpling using your thumb and forefinger to hold it and ease the filling in up to the edge of the egg pastry. Place on your work surface to flatten the base (they will look like a small cylinder-like dumpling). Lightly press a small round of white shallot into the top of each dumpling.

3 Make a doily with baking paper (cut small holes in a circle of paper) and line a steamer with it.

4 Place a batch of siu mai in the steamer, leaving space in between each. Steam for 8 mins over simmering water. Serve dumplings hot, with chilli sauce, if desired. Repeat with the remaining dumplings.

An extremely versatile dish, plain 'jook' lends itself to many different flavours and uses. Commonly served plain as a breakfast dish with store-bought 'yau tiu' (Chinese fried dough strips). Or when feeling a bit off food, a bowl of plain 'jook' can do wonders. It gives the body a chance to cleanse itself.

Jook ~ Congee *or* Rice Porridge

SERVES 2–3

1 cup short grain rice, rinsed
5 cups water or chicken stock*
4 slices ginger

Salt and pepper
Sesame oil, to serve
1 green shallot (green onion / scallion), sliced, to serve

1 Boil the rice, water or stock and ginger over high heat until the rice grains have broken up. Add more water if necessary, to continue cooking until the rice is mushy. Lower the heat and simmer until the rice looks creamy.

2 Serve plain jook (congee) with your choice of condiments e.g. salted duck eggs (store-bought), ikan bilis with peanuts (see page 59), preserved salted vegetables e.g. olives, hot radishes, etc. (normally for breakfast).
Or if making gai jook (chicken congee) as a light meal, see recipe below.

3 Season to taste with salt, pepper and sesame oil. Garnish with shallots.

*See 'Basics' on page 167 for how to make homemade chicken stock.

Gai Jook ~ Congee *with* Chicken

SERVES 2–3

300 g (10½ oz) chicken breast fillet, sliced
1 tsp salt
½ tsp pepper
1 tsp cornflour (cornstarch)
2 Tbsp water
1 Tbsp oil
4 slices ginger

Salt and pepper
Sesame oil, to serve
1 green shallot (green onion / scallion), sliced, to serve

1 Marinate the sliced chicken in the seasoning ingredients (salt, pepper, cornflour, water, oil, ginger). Mix well and set aside.

2 When ready to serve, heat up the jook (congee), add in the marinated chicken meat, stir to loosen and let it cook for 5 mins, or until the chicken is opaque and cooked.

3 Season to taste with salt and pepper. Serve up in individual bowls, add a dash of sesame oil and garnish with shallots.

Lo Mein ~ Tossed Egg Noodles *with* Oyster Sauce

These noodles could be served as a side with 'jook' (congee, see page 43) or as a light meal with your choice of meat e.g. soya sauce chicken (see page 87), 'cha siew' (BBQ pork, see page 88), etc.

SERVES 2

220 g (7¾ oz) fresh egg noodles
1 Tbsp oyster sauce
1 Tbsp soy sauce
1 Tbsp dark soy sauce
½ Tbsp sesame oil
1 Tbsp oil
Asian greens, to serve
1 green shallot (green onion / scallion), finely sliced, to garnish

1 Bring 2–3 litres of water to the boil in a large saucepan.

2 Put in the egg noodles. Cook for 3–5 mins or until al dente. Use a pair of chopsticks to loosen the strands of noodles. Using a spider strainer, scoop the noodles out and into a basin of cold water. Swirl the noodles around to wash off the starch or rinse under the tap. Scoop up and quickly submerge the noodles back in the pot of boiling water for about 30 secs. Scoop out, drain well.

3 Put the sauces and oils in a mixing bowl. Add the noodles to the bowl and toss well.

4 Plate up with some steamed or blanched Asian greens e.g. gai lan or bok choy. Garnish with shallots.

Wonton ~ Short Soup Dumplings

This is one of the most frequently requested dishes by my grandchildren. I like to make extra when the pork is really fresh at my butcher, then freeze them uncooked.

SERVES 4

Meat Marinade

¾ tsp salt

1 tsp sugar

2 tsp cornflour (cornstarch)

¼ tsp white pepper* (optional)

½ tsp chicken stock powder

1 tsp sesame oil

1 tsp cooking oil

50 mL (1¾ fl oz) water

250–300 g (8¾–10½ oz) pork mince or chicken mince

1 packet wonton wrappers (e.g. Double Merino brand)

Chicken broth or wonton soup, to serve (optional)

1 Mix the marinade ingredients together in a mixing bowl.

2 Add the mince and stir to combine well. Stir the mixture until it becomes sticky. Add a bit more water if the mixture looks dry. Set aside for 20 mins.

3 Place ½ tsp – 1 tsp of meat mixture in the centre of the wrapper, fold in half and crimp / gather the edges. Repeat with the rest of the wrappers.

4 Bring a large pot of water to the boil. Add in the wontons 8–10 at a time. The wontons will float when cooked. Leave to cook for a further 1 min. Remove with a spider strainer and transfer to chicken broth or wonton soup, or have them dry with a soy and garlic oil dressing. Cook the rest of the wontons.

*Young children might find the white pepper too hot for their liking. Omit, if necessary.

LIGHT MEALS

Loh Bak Goh ~ White Radish Cake

When you order 'loh bak goh' at yum cha or dim sum restaurants, they panfry small pieces for you in their trolley carts. It is served with condiments such as sesame peanut sauce or hoisin sauce. At home, I like to make it with more shrimps, 'larp cheong', mushrooms and 'loh bak', and serve it with chilli sauce.

SERVES 4

1 Tbsp oil

40 g (1⅜ oz) dried shrimps (har mei), washed, soaked to soften, diced

2 (80 g, 2⅞ oz) larp cheong (Chinese sausages), diced

2–3 (40 g, 1⅜ oz) dried shiitake mushrooms, rehydrated, diced

Salt and pepper

1 kg (2 lb 3 oz) loh bak (white radish / Chinese turnip / daikon), peeled, grated or shredded

1 cup (250 mL) water

2 tsp sugar

250 g (8¾ oz) rice flour (not glutinous)

2 tsp salt

¼ tsp white pepper

1 tsp chicken stock powder

1 Tbsp sesame seeds, toasted*

1 green shallot (green onion / scallion), chopped

Chilli sauce, to serve (optional)

*To toast sesame seeds: dry fry the seeds in a frypan over low heat until lightly toasted.

1 Grease a deep 20 cm (8") or 23 cm (9") round pan.

2 Heat the oil in a wok. Stir-fry the shrimps, larp cheong and mushrooms, taking care not to burn the larp cheong. Add salt and pepper to taste. Dish up and set aside.

3 Boil the radish in 1 cup of water until soft (the radish will release some water). Add in the 2 tsp sugar. Drain the cooking liquid from the radish and measure the volume. If the cooking liquid is less than 1½ cups, add some water to make up the difference. If it's more than 1½ cups liquid, discard the excess. Return the 1½ cups liquid to the cooked radish. Transfer to a large mixing bowl.

4 Put the rice flour in and mix with the radish mixture while it's still hot. Stir well to form a pasty mixture. Add in the stir-fried shrimps, larp cheong and mushrooms, as well as the salt, white pepper and chicken powder. Mix in with a wooden spoon.

5 Pour the radish mixture into the greased pan. Smooth the top. Steam on high heat for 1 hour. Replenish the steaming water when low. Test with a skewer — if the mixture does not stick, it's done. Remove from heat and sprinkle the surface with the sesame seeds and shallots. Cool completely in the pan.

6 Remove from the pan and wrap in cling wrap. Store in the fridge if not eating that day.

7 To serve, cut into slices and panfry until lightly browned on both sides. Serve with chilli sauce, if desired.

Facing page features a Chinese hand painted tile and bamboo trivet from Nanna Brab (1960s)

Woo Tau Goh ~ Taro Cake

This is one of the dishes that my mother-in-law would often make when we would "come home" and visit her at her house. Her method and ingredients were very approximate and done by sight or touch. Over the years I have got it to a flavour and consistency that I like.

SERVES 4

600 g (1 lb 5 oz) woo tau (taro)
2 dried shiitake mushrooms, rehydrated
2 larp cheong (Chinese sausages)
½ piece of cured pork belly (larb yoke) (optional)
25 g (⅞ oz) dried shrimps (har mei), soaked
500 mL (17 fl oz) water
1 green shallot (green onion / scallion), chopped
1 Tbsp sesame seeds, toasted*
Chilli sauce, to serve

Seasonings

1 tsp chicken stock powder
1½ tsp 5-spice powder^
1 tsp sugar
1½ tsp salt
¼ tsp white pepper
1½ tsp sesame oil

Flour Mixture

180 g (6⅜ oz) rice flour (not glutinous)
1 Tbsp cornflour (cornstarch)
250 mL (8½ fl oz) water

1 Peel the taro and dice into 1 cm (⅜") cubes. Finely dice the mushrooms, larp cheong and cured belly pork (if using). Roughly chop the dried shrimps. Set aside.

2 Heat a wok or pan on medium heat. Add the larp cheong and pork and stir-fry for 2 mins. Add the taro, mushrooms and shrimps. Cook for 3 mins, stir to combine well. Add the seasonings and 500 mL water. Cover, turn heat to low and simmer for 6–8 mins. Uncover, turn off heat. Cool slightly.

3 Mix the rice flour, cornflour and 250 mL water in a large mixing bowl until smooth. Add the taro mixture (no need to wait for it to cool completely) to the flour mixture. Mix thoroughly until it thickens to a cement-like paste.

4 Grease 2 x 20 cm (8") round pans or 1 large deep 23 cm (9") round pan. Pour the taro mixture into the pan(s). Smooth and level the top.

5 Steam for 40 mins (small pans); 60–90 mins (large pan). Replenish the water during steaming. Test with a skewer. If it comes out clean, it's done. Remove from heat and sprinkle the top with green shallots and sesame seeds. Leave to cool in the pan.

6 Turn the taro cake out from the pan. Slice the taro cake into 1 cm x 5 cm (⅜" x 2") pieces and panfry the slices until lightly browned. Serve with chilli sauce.

*To toast sesame seeds: dry fry the seeds in a frypan over low heat until lightly toasted.
^See 'Basics' on page 166 for how to make your own 5-spice powder.

Facing page features Nanna Brab's Royal Albert fine china tea set and Jeanie's homemade larb yoke

Snake Beans *with* Dried Shrimps

SERVES 4

20 g (¾ oz) dried shrimps (har mei)

1 bunch snake beans (long beans), cut into 4 cm (1½") lengths

1 Tbsp oil

2 cloves garlic, minced

2 tsp oyster sauce

¼ tsp salt

¼ tsp sugar

1–2 Tbsp water

1 long red chilli, sliced

1. Rinse the dried shrimps. Soak for 30 mins. Drain and set aside.

2. Bring a pot of water to the boil. Blanch the beans for 2 mins. Remove and plunge in cold water to stop them from cooking further. Drain.

3. Heat a wok or pan over medium heat. Add the oil, cook the shrimps and garlic for 30 secs. Add in the snake beans, oyster sauce, salt and sugar and stir everything until well combined. Add in some water. Cook for 1–2 mins, then toss in the sliced chilli.

4. Dish up. Serve as a side or shared dish.

Fried Kang Kong Belachan

SERVES 4–6

2 bunches kang kong (ong choy, water spinach)

20 g (¾ oz) dried shrimps (har mei)

15 g (½ oz) belachan (dried shrimp paste)

4 cloves garlic

3 red shallots (eschalots), chopped (optional)

1 long red chilli, sliced

4 Tbsp oil

2 Tbsp soy sauce

1 tsp sugar, or to taste

1 fresh red chilli, sliced, for garnish

1 Remove the old stalks from the kang kong, snap into 5 cm (2") lengths. Wash and drain.

2 Soak the dried shrimps in hot water for 10–15 mins, drain.

3 Wrap belachan in foil and toast in the frypan for 2 mins each side. Set aside to cool in the foil.

4 Pound the garlic, red shallots (if using), chilli, shrimps and belachan in a mortar and pestle into a rough paste, or blend in a small food processor.

5 Heat the oil in a wok, add the spice paste and fry until fragrant. Add the kang kong and stir-fry, mixing it into the spice mixture. Do this until the kang kong starts to wilt. Add the soy sauce and sugar and toss everything together. Add in the sliced chilli and stir-fry for 30 secs. Turn off heat.

6 Dish up. Serve as a side or shared dish.

Rice *and* Noodles

Fried Rice *with* Prawns *and* Larp Cheong

SERVES 6

2 Tbsp cooking oil
4 eggs, lightly beaten
4 Tbsp cooking oil
½ onion, sliced
2 cloves garlic, minced
150 g (5¼ oz) raw prawns
2 larp cheong (Chinese sausages), diced or sliced into rounds
1 cup frozen peas, or peas & corn
1 cup carrots, diced
4 cups cooked rice*

Seasoning

1 Tbsp light soy sauce
1 Tbsp oyster sauce, or 1 tsp chicken stock powder
½ tsp salt, or to taste
⅛ tsp pepper, or to taste
1 Tbsp dark soy sauce (for colour)

Garnish (optional)

2 green shallots (green onions / scallions), chopped
2 Tbsp fried shallots^ (fried onions)
Fresh chilli, sliced

1 Heat 2 Tbsp oil in a wok. Pour in the beaten eggs, swirling to coat the bottom in a circle. Fry the eggs until cooked, turn over once and shred the eggs with a wok chan (metal spatula). Remove and set aside.

2 Reheat the wok and add 4 Tbsp oil to fry the onions and garlic until fragrant. Add the prawns and larp cheong and stir-fry for a minute or so (watch that the larp cheong doesn't get burnt).

3 Add in the peas and carrots. Cook for 1 min.

4 Stir in the cooked rice and mix in the seasonings. Return the cooked shredded eggs to the wok and mix well.

5 Dish up onto plates and garnish with green shallots and fried shallots. Serve chilli on the side, if desired.

Note: A good fried rice should have separate grains of rice and not be mushy.

*Precook the rice several hours before frying; 2 cups of uncooked rice will make 4 cups of cooked rice. Or use leftover rice.

^See 'Basics' on page 166 for how to make fried shallots (eschalots).

Hainanese Chicken Rice

Popular in Malaysia, this is a truly versatile dish that can be enjoyed at lunch, dinner, supper, or any time of day.

SERVES 4–6

1.2 kg – 1.4 kg (2 lb 10 oz – 3 lb) free range chicken (whole)

2 tsp salt

3 green shallots (green onions / scallions), knotted

3–5 slices ginger, cut 0.5 cm (¼") thick

2 cloves garlic, bashed

Rice

2 Tbsp chicken fat (reserved from whole chicken), or oil

2 cloves garlic, minced

2 slices ginger, cut 0.5 cm (¼") thick

3 cups jasmine rice, washed and drained

2 pandan leaves (screwpine leaves), knotted

4½ cups poaching liquid (reserved from whole chicken)

Shallot & Ginger Sauce

4 green shallots (green onions / scallions), finely sliced

5 cm (2") piece ginger, peeled, finely grated

¼ tsp salt

¼ tsp chicken stock powder

4 Tbsp cooking oil

Garlic & Chilli Sauce

3 cloves garlic, peeled, roughly chopped

3 long red chillies, roughly chopped

4 Tbsp vinegar

4 Tbsp sugar

¼ tsp salt

3 tsp sesame oil

1 Lebanese cucumber, sliced

2 sprigs coriander (cilantro), for garnish

1 Fill a large pot (tall enough to fit the chicken) with water. Bring to the boil.

2 Clean the chicken and cut off any excess fat. Reserve the chicken fat for the rice.

3 Rub the salt into the chicken cavity. Stuff the green shallots, ginger and garlic into the cavity.

4 Place the chicken, breast side up, into the pot of boiling water. Bring it back to the boil, then lower the heat and cover with a lid. Do not let the water simmer, it should be still. Poach the chicken for 50–60 mins. Reserve 4½ cups poaching liquid for the rice.

5 To cook the rice, heat a frypan on medium heat. Put in the chicken fat to render. When the pieces of fat have shrunk, remove and discard. Add in extra oil if there is not enough chicken fat (2 Tbsp). Then add in the garlic and ginger, sauté until lightly browned. Then add the rice, stir-fry for 5 mins, coating the rice in the fat.

6 Put the rice and pandan leaves in a rice cooker. Add the reserved poaching liquid in. Cook the rice.

7 Make the sauces:

Shallot & Ginger Sauce

Combine the green shallots, ginger, salt and chicken powder in a bowl. Heat the oil in a small saucepan over high heat. Pour it over the ginger and shallots. Mix and set aside.

Garlic & Chilli Sauce

Blitz the ingredients with a stick blender until smooth.

8 Remove the chicken from the stock and submerge it in a basin of cold water. When cooled, drain. Rub sesame oil all over the chicken.

9 To serve, debone the chicken and slice into 2 cm (¾") pieces. Cut the cucumber into slices and place on a plate alongside the chicken. Garnish with sprigs of coriander. Serve with the chicken rice and sauces.

Nasi Lemak ~ Coconut Rice

A fragrant rice cooked with coconut and pandan, to be served alongside simple sides or more complex curries.

SERVES 4

Coconut Rice

1½ cups white rice
2 slices ginger
1–2 cloves garlic, peeled
2–3 pandan leaves (screwpine leaves), knotted
125 mL (½ cup) coconut cream
½ tsp salt

1 Wash and rinse the rice till the water is clear. Drain

2 Put the rice, ginger, garlic and pandan leaves in a rice cooker. Add the coconut cream and salt and top up with water to come up 2 cm (¾") above the level of the rice. Cook rice until dry, use a rice scoop to loosen the rice grains. Stand for 10–15 mins.

3 Keep warm until ready to serve with ikan bilis and sambal (as pictured, see facing page for recipes), or with curry chicken (see page 117; 118), or beef rendang (see page 121), etc.

Ikan Bilis ~ Dried Anchovies

50 g (1¾ oz) ikan bilis, degutted
½ cup oil
1 cup raw peanuts
1 Tbsp caster sugar (superfine sugar)

1   If the ikan bilis are very salty, rinse them and then dry in the sun for 1 hour.

2   Heat the oil in a small pan over medium heat. Test by putting in a piece of ikan bilis. The oil is hot enough when rapid bubbles appear around the ikan bilis.

3   Deep fry the peanuts in oil until golden brown. Remove and drain on paper towel.

4   Fry the ikan bilis in 2 batches until golden and crispy. Scoop out and drain on a sieve lined with paper towel. Set aside. Repeat with the remaining ikan bilis. Cool.

5   Combine the cooled peanuts and ikan bilis in a bowl and sprinkle with the sugar. Serve as a side with nasi lemak or jook (see page 43).

Tip: Raw peanuts could be roasted in the oven or slowly pan roasted^, instead of deep frying.

Ikan Bilis Sambal

3 Tbsp oil
1 medium onion, sliced
2 red chillies, deseeded and finely chopped
2 Tbsp tamarind puree
4 Tbsp water
1 Tbsp sugar
50 g (1¾ oz) crispy ikan bilis (dried anchovies)
50 g (1¾ oz) roasted peanuts^

1   Heat the oil in a pan. Add the onion and chilli and fry until the onion softens. Add in the tamarind puree, water and sugar. Simmer until the sauce thickens slightly. Turn off the heat. Cool.

2   Stir in the ikan bilis and peanuts. Serve as a side with nasi lemak.

Prawn Sambal

10 dried red chillies, soaked
10 red shallots (eschalots)
1–2 cloves garlic
5 g (⅛ oz) fresh turmeric, sliced
1 stalk (30 g, 1 oz) lemongrass, white part only, sliced
20 g (¾ oz) belachan (dried shrimp paste), toasted*
5 Tbsp oil
10 g (⅜ oz) tamarind pulp
250 mL (8½ fl oz) water
¼ tsp salt
3 Tbsp sugar
500 g (1 lb 2 oz) raw prawns

1   Pound the chillies, red shallots, garlic, turmeric, lemongrass and belachan in a mortar and pestle, or blend in a small food processor.

2   Heat the oil in a wok and sauté the spices until fragrant, about 10–15 mins.

3   Mix the tamarind pulp with the water in a bowl. Use your fingers to loosen the pulp.

4   Strain the tamarind mixture (discard the pulp). Add the tamarind liquid to the wok with the salt and sugar. Bring it to the boil.

5   Add the prawns, stir, and bring the sauce to the boil again. Dish up. Serve as a shared main or as a side for nasi lemak.

*See 'Basics' on page 167 for how to prepare toasted belachan. Alternatively, some Asian supermarkets stock pre-toasted belachan (e.g. Jeeny's brand).
^See 'Basics' on page 167 for how to roast peanuts.

Jee Par Farn ~ Pork Chop Rice

A wholesome dish comprised of vegetables, protein and carbohydrates. Serve it in the hot baking dish, straight from the oven to the table.

SERVES 4

1 kg (2 lb 3 oz) pork loin chops*
2 tsp sugar
1 tsp salt
¼ tsp pepper
2 cloves garlic, minced
2 Tbsp oil
2 Tbsp sherry

Fried Rice

2 Tbsp oil
2 eggs, lightly beaten
½ onion, diced
1 small carrot, diced
2 cups cooked rice
1 cup frozen peas & corn
½ tsp salt
Soy sauce, to taste

Sauce

½ cup (125 mL) vinegar
1 cup (250 mL) water
2 Tbsp tomato paste
2 Tbsp sugar, or to taste
1 Tbsp Worcestershire sauce
1 red or brown onion, sliced
2 cloves garlic, minced
1 Tbsp oil
4 medium tomatoes, quartered
2 tsp cornflour (cornstarch), mixed with 2 Tbsp water

1   Trim the pork loin chops. Combine the sugar, salt, pepper, garlic, oil and sherry in a mixing bowl. Add in the pork chops and mix well. Leave to marinate overnight in the fridge.

2   For the fried rice, heat 1 Tbsp oil in a wok over medium-high heat. Add the beaten eggs in and scramble them, cutting them into pieces with a wok chan (metal turner). Remove and set aside.

3   Add the remaining oil and cook the onions and diced carrot for 1 min. Add the rice and the frozen vegetables and toss all the ingredients until well incorporated. Add the cooked egg back in and toss again. Season the rice with salt and soy sauce. Scoop the rice into a baking dish.

4   In a large frypan over medium-high heat, brown the pork chops on both sides. Lay them on top of the rice.

5   Preheat oven to 160°C (320°F).

6   To make the sauce; mix the vinegar, water, tomato paste, sugar and Worcestershire sauce together in a bowl. Fry the onions and garlic in 1 Tbsp oil in a saucepan. Add in the cut tomatoes and the vinegar mixture. Bring to the boil. Season to taste; the sauce should be a bit tangy and sweet. Thicken the sauce with the cornflour mixture and pour it over the pork chops in the baking dish. Cover with foil and bake in preheated oven for 45 mins.

7   Serve with some greens e.g. steamed green beans, or sautéed spinach, if desired.

Tips:
Prepare and marinate the pork the night before for a fuller flavour.
Precook the rice several hours before frying; 1 cup of uncooked rice makes 2 cups of cooked rice. Or use leftover rice.

*Look for pork loin chops that are not too thick, 1–1.5 cm (½"). Otherwise, increase the cooking time to compensate.

Char Kway Teow ~ Stir Fried Flat Rice Noodles

A popular street-food in Malaysia and Singapore. In the past, vendors set up stalls at night in front of shopfronts, or operated food carts in the night markets. Some vendors even set up small eating areas with wooden benches and stools for you to quickly enjoy your supper and go.

SERVES 2

3 Tbsp oil

6–8 raw prawns, peeled and deveined

1 clove garlic, finely chopped

1 larp cheong (Chinese sausage), sliced 6 mm (¼") thick

100 g (3½ oz) fried fish cake, sliced

250 g (9 oz) hor fun (flat rice noodles), sliced 2 cm (¾") thick

50 mL (2 fl oz) water

2 eggs, lightly beaten or whole

Handful of bean sprouts

5–6 stalks gow choy (garlic chives), cut into 5 cm (2") lengths

Fresh chilli or sambal chilli, to serve

Sauce

2 Tbsp light soy sauce

1 Tbsp dark soy caramel (thick soya sauce), or ABC kecap manis (sweet soy sauce)

1 Tbsp oyster sauce

2 tsp sugar

¼ tsp white pepper

1 Mix the sauce ingredients together in a small bowl and set aside.

2 Heat 2 Tbsp oil in a wok. Stir-fry the prawns with the garlic for 30 secs, remove and set aside.

3 Add in the larp cheong and the fish cake. Stir-fry over medium-low heat. Careful not to burn the larp cheong.

4 Add in the hor fun and the sauce. Turn the heat up to high and toss the noodles so that they are evenly coated with the sauce. Sprinkle 50 mL water onto the noodles. When the noodles are soft, push them to one side of the wok.

5 Put the remaining 1 Tbsp oil in the centre of the wok, crack the eggs in, give it a stir and cover the eggs with the noodles for 30 secs before starting to stir-fry again.

6 Add in the cooked prawns, bean sprouts and garlic chives and give it a final toss to mix in. Dish up and serve, with fresh chilli or sambal chilli.

Mee Goreng ~ Hawker Style Fried Noodles

In Malaysia in the 1960s, I remember seeing hawkers pushing their food carts around, or riding their tricycles with food carts attached. These street vendors would set up their food carts and mobile stalls by the side of the road and cook your noodles to order. There are many different styles of 'mee goreng', or fried noodles. I remember the Indian-style best from my younger years, and this is the style that I cook at home.

SERVES 3–4

2½ Tbsp cooking oil

2 cloves garlic, minced

1 Tbsp chilli paste, or fresh chillies (optional)

3–4 pieces fried bean curd (tofu), cut 1 cm (⅜") thick

1 potato (150 g, 5¼ oz) boiled, sliced ½ cm (¼") thick

4 small squid, cut into rings or ½ cm (¼") strips

300 g (10½ oz) yellow (Hokkien) noodles, rinsed and drained

½ cup water

2 large eggs, lightly beaten

150 g (5¼ oz) bean sprouts, rinsed and drained

Lettuce leaves, to garnish

Lime wedges, to serve

Sauce

2 Tbsp kecap manis (sweet soy sauce) (e.g. ABC brand)

2 Tbsp soy sauce

3 Tbsp tomato sauce (ketchup)

1 Tbsp sugar

1. Mix the sauce ingredients together in a bowl.

2. Heat the wok on medium-high heat. Add 2 Tbsp oil, garlic, chilli paste or chillies (if using), bean curd, potatoes and squid. Stir-fry until fragrant.

3. Add the yellow noodles and the sauce. Continue stirring and mixing with a wok chan (metal turner) until the noodles are softened, adding a small amount of water at a time to cook the noodles. Lower the heat, push the noodles to the side of the wok.

4. Put the remaining oil in the wok. Add the eggs in, scramble them with the wok chan and cover with the noodles for 1 min. Then add the bean sprouts and give it a quick stir.

5. Dish up and garnish with some lettuce leaves and lime wedges. Squeeze lime juice over the noodles before serving.

Singapore Noodles

In Singapore, there is no such thing as 'Singapore Noodles'! In fact, growing up, my family called it 'Fried Bee Hoon' and it was made with very hot chilli, not curry powder. These noodles have been renamed and popularised in Australia.

SERVES 2–3

200 g (7 oz) dried rice vermicelli (mei fun)

3 Tbsp oil

2 eggs, lightly beaten

2–3 cloves garlic, minced

½ medium onion, sliced

200 g (7 oz) chicken, sliced (or cha siew, or ham)

8–10 raw prawns, peeled and deveined

½ cup water

½ red capsicum (pepper), sliced

4–5 green beans, sliced diagonally

½ carrot, julienned

3 green shallots (green onions / scallions), cut into 2.5 cm (1") lengths

Sauce

2 Tbsp soy sauce

2 Tbsp cooking wine, e.g. sherry or sake

2 Tbsp curry powder (e.g. Clive of India or Keens brands)

½ tsp sugar

½ tsp pepper (optional)

1 tsp chicken stock powder

1 Soak the dried rice vermicelli for 1 hour. Drain.

2 Mix the sauce ingredients together in a small bowl. Set aside.

3 Heat 1 Tbsp oil in a wok. Pour in the beaten eggs and swirl them around the wok to make a thin omelette. Flip and cook the other side. Remove and set aside to cool down. Roll up and cut into shreds.

4 Put the remaining 2 Tbsp oil in the wok, stir-fry the garlic and onion for 1 min. Add in the chicken and prawns. Cook until the chicken changes colour.

5 Add in the rice vermicelli and spoon in half the sauce. Stir the noodles and meat together. Add the rest of the sauce and mix in well. Test the texture of the noodles. If it's not soft add a small amount of water at a time. It should still have a bite to it (al dente).

6 Finally, add in the capsicum, beans, carrots, sliced omelette and green shallots. Toss through the noodles. Season to taste. Dish up and serve.

....

Variations:

Other vegetables e.g. celery, cabbage, would also go well.

The eggs could also be scrambled in the wok in step 3, instead of making a thin omelette.

Zha Jeung Mein
~ Beijing Spicy Sauce Noodles

There are many versions of 'Beijing Noodles'. In Beijing, it is really spicy. This is my version.

SERVES 5–6

- 3 Tbsp oil
- 2 onions, finely chopped
- 2 cloves garlic, minced
- 800 g (1 lb 12 oz) pork mince
- 100 g (3½ oz) fresh shiitake mushrooms, or spiced pressed tofu, diced (optional)
- 50 g (1¾ oz) brown bean paste, or miso paste
- 20 g (¾ oz) sweet bean paste, or hoisin sauce
- 1 Tbsp chilli bean paste (optional)
- 1 Tbsp dark soy sauce
- 1 Tbsp Shaoxing wine, or cooking wine
- 2 Tbsp sugar
- 1 tsp chicken stock powder
- 2 Tbsp tomato paste
- 1½ cups water
- 1½ packets (750 g, 1 lb 10 oz) Shanghai noodles, or yang chuen noodles
- 2 cups carrots, shredded
- 2 cups cucumber, julienned
- 2 cups purple or white cabbage, shredded
- 1 small packet preserved mustard stems
- Sesame seeds, toasted*
- 1 green shallot (green onion / scallion), finely sliced

1 Put the oil in a large saucepan on medium-high heat. Fry the onion and garlic for 1 min, or until the onion is softened. Add the pork mince and cook for 5–10 mins, stirring and breaking up any lumps, until the mince changes colour. Add the mushrooms or tofu cubes, if using.

2 Add the bean pastes and stir to coat the mince. Omit the chilli bean paste if you wish (for children). Then add the dark soy, wine, sugar, chicken powder, tomato paste and water. Mix and stir in well. Reduce the heat to medium and simmer for 20–30 mins or until the sauce thickens.

3 Meanwhile, bring a large pot of water to the boil, then add the noodles and cook for 4–5 mins. Drain in a colander and shake off the excess water.

4 Divide the noodles among serving bowls. Top with the pork mince sauce, carrots, cucumber and cabbage garnishes. Put 1–2 teaspoons of preserved mustard stems on top of the pork mince. Sprinkle with sesame seeds and sliced green shallots.

*To toast sesame seeds: dry fry the seeds in a frypan over low heat until lightly toasted.

Pad Thai

A popular stir-fried noodle dish that is family-friendly. Many cooks would have their own variation; this is mine.

SERVES 2

300 g (10½ oz) dried Thai rice stick noodles, soaked 15–20 mins

1 Tbsp dried shrimps, soaked 10 mins

3 Tbsp oil

100 g (3 ½ oz) chicken tenderloin, sliced

2 garlic cloves, minced

80 g (1 cup) hard tofu, cut into small pieces

90 mL (3 fl oz) chicken stock or water

2 eggs, lightly beaten

3 Tbsp roasted peanuts^, chopped

Handful of gow choy (garlic chives), cut into 2 cm (¾") lengths

1 cup bean sprouts

Lime wedges, to serve

Dried chilli flakes, or fresh chilli, sliced, to serve (optional)

Sauce

3 Tbsp fish sauce

1 Tbsp soy sauce

1 Tbsp oyster sauce

2 Tbsp tamarind puree

3 Tbsp sugar

1 Mix the sauce ingredients together in a small bowl. Drain the rice noodles and dried shrimps.

2 Heat the oil in a wok on medium heat. Add the chicken and stir-fry quickly. Add the shrimps, garlic and tofu and stir-fry until the garlic turns light brown. Add the drained noodles. Keep stirring over high heat. Add the chicken stock or water and stir-fry until the noodles are soft.

3 Turn the heat down, add the sauce ingredients and stir well to combine.

4 Push the noodles to the side of the wok. Add a bit of oil (if needed), add the eggs and stir to break up the yolks, then combine with the noodles. Add the peanuts and garlic chives. Stir. Taste and adjust seasoning.

5 Lastly, add the bean sprouts and toss in quickly with the noodles for 30 secs. Turn off the heat and dish up.

6 Serve garnished with lime wedges and chilli flakes or fresh chillies, if desired.

^See 'Basics' on page 167 for how to roast peanuts.

Jap Chae ~ Korean Sweet Potato Noodles

SERVES 4–5

300 g (10½ oz) pork scotch fillet, or pork shoulder
½ tsp salt
Dash of pepper
2 tsp sesame oil

300 g (10½ oz) Korean sweet potato noodles
1 Tbsp sesame oil

4 Tbsp light soy sauce
2 Tbsp oyster sauce
1 tsp chicken stock powder

2 Tbsp cooking oil
6–8 dried shiitake mushrooms (soaked in hot water 30 mins), or 100–150 g (3½–5 oz) fresh shiitake mushrooms, thinly sliced
3 cloves garlic, minced
2 medium carrots, julienned
½ red capsicum (pepper), sliced
100 g (3½ oz) snow peas, or green beans, or spinach, sliced
3 green shallots (green onions / scallions), sliced diagonally
1 Tbsp sesame seeds, toasted*

1 Cut the pork into strips. Marinate with salt, pepper and 2 tsp sesame oil. Set aside.

2 Bring a large pot of water to the boil. Put in the sweet potato noodles and boil until the noodles are cooked through. Drain. Rinse in cold water to refresh. Drain again. Cut the noodles into 15–20 cm (6–8") lengths. Place the noodles in a large bowl and mix in 1 Tbsp sesame oil. Set aside.

3 Mix the light soy sauce, oyster sauce and chicken powder together in a bowl. Set aside.

4 Heat 2 Tbsp cooking oil in a frypan or skillet over medium heat. Stir-fry the marinated pork, mushrooms and garlic for 1 min, until the pork changes colour. Add in the carrots, capsicum, snow peas and green shallots. Stir-fry for 1 min. Add in the seasoning sauce, mix in. Remove from heat.

5 Transfer the cooked ingredients to the noodles. Toss gently with your hands until combined, loosening the noodles.

6 Transfer the mixed noodles to a large platter and garnish with toasted sesame seeds. Serve as a shared dish.

*To toast sesame seeds: dry fry the seeds in a frypan over low heat until lightly toasted.

To make it a vegetarian dish, omit the pork, oyster sauce and chicken stock powder. You may like to replace the pork with hard tofu, cut into strips. Add a bit of salt or mushroom soy sauce back to replace the oyster sauce. Replace the chicken stock powder with vegetable stock powder.

Kari Laksa Lemak ~ Malaysian Curry Laksa

SERVES 6

1.5 kg (3 lb 5 oz) whole chicken
8 cups (2 litres) water
⅓ cup (80 mL) oil
3 sprigs curry leaves
3 slices galangal, cut 2 cm (¾") thick
1 x 400 mL (13½ fl oz) can coconut milk
1 packet fried tofu puffs (tau foo pok), halved
18 fresh green prawns, shelled and deveined
1 packet bean sprouts
1 packet (400 g, 14 oz) dried rice vermicelli (mei fun), soaked
1 packet (500 g, 1 lb 2 oz) fresh yellow (Hokkien) noodles
1 packet (180 g, 6⅜ oz) fried fish cake, sliced
Mint leaves, to garnish
Lime wedges, to garnish
Chilli sambal, to garnish

Spice Paste

10 shallots (eschalots), or 1 brown onion
3 stalks lemongrass, white part only
6 candlenuts or macadamias, smashed
6 dried red chillies, soaked, deseeded, chopped
6 fresh red chillies, deseeded, chopped
2 cm (¾") piece fresh turmeric, or 1 tsp turmeric powder
1 Tbsp coriander powder
4 cloves garlic, peeled and smashed
4 Tbsp dried shrimps (har mei), soaked
10 g (⅜ oz) belachan (dried shrimp paste), toasted*

1 Wash and clean the chicken, remove any excess fat. Boil 8 cups of water in a large stock pot. Put the whole chicken in and cook on medium heat for 40 mins. Remove the chicken and cool. Reserve the chicken water. Shred the meat and set aside.

2 Put the spice paste ingredients in a food processor and blend to a paste.

3 Heat the oil in a pan on medium heat. Put in the blended spice paste, curry leaves (removed from the centre stems) and galangal slices and fry slowly until the laksa paste is fragrant and the oil separates — about 20 mins.

4 Add the laksa paste to the chicken water in the stock pot and bring to a boil. Lower the heat and simmer for 10 mins.

5 Add in the coconut milk and tofu puffs. Stir and keep the soup on a simmer until ready to serve.

6 Boil some more water in a large saucepan. Blanch the prawns, remove, set aside. Blanch the bean sprouts, remove, set aside.

7 Put a handful of rice vermicelli and yellow noodles in a noodle strainer basket in the boiling water and blanch for 30 secs. Drain off the excess water and transfer to a noodle bowl. Top with bean sprouts, prawns, shredded chicken and slices of fish cake.

8 Scoop hot laksa soup and tofu puffs over the noodles. Garnish with mint, lime and chilli sambal. Repeat for the other bowls.

*See 'Basics' on page 167 for how to prepare toasted belachan. Alternatively, some Asian supermarkets stock pre-toasted belachan (e.g. Jeeny's brand).

'Laksa' (pronounced "luck-SAA") has grown in popularity and is available in many forms and variations. This here is an authentic, full-flavoured Malaysian laksa. It is satisfying, creamy and spicy. If you like it more spicy, you can add more chillies to the spice paste.

A Malaysian dish that utilises prawn heads to give the soup a rich flavour. So remember to keep your prawn head peelings and store in the freezer for future use. This dish is usually served with kang kong and bean sprouts to complement the noodle soup, however, the meat and seafood garnishes are interchangeable.

Har Meen ~ Prawn Noodle Soup

SERVES 6

Soup Base Stock

2 Tbsp oil
2 cloves garlic, peeled
1 onion, sliced
500 g (1 lb 2 oz) prawn heads
8 cups (2 litres) water
2 chicken carcasses (chicken frames)

Noodles and Garnishes

500 g (1 lb 2 oz) fresh prawns
1 packet (180 g, 6⅜ oz) fried fish cake
3 hard-boiled eggs
1 pork fillet, or chicken breast (approx. 300 g, 10½ oz)
1 packet (500 g, 1 lb 2 oz) bean sprouts
1 bunch kang kong (water spinach, ong choy), or English spinach
1 packet (500 g, 1 lb 2 oz) fresh yellow (Hokkien) noodles
½ packet (200–250g, 7–8¾ oz) dried rice vermicelli (mei fun), soaked in water
Crispy fried shallots* (fried onions)
Chilli paste (see recipe below)

Chilli Paste

10 dried long red chillies, deseeded and soaked
5 fresh long red chillies, deseeded
2 brown onions, finely chopped
20 dried shrimps (har mei), soaked in water 15–20 mins
4 cloves garlic, minced
½ cup oil
2 Tbsp sugar
1 tsp salt

*See 'Basics' on page 166 for how to make fried shallots (eschalots)

Soup Base Stock

1 Heat oil in a large saucepan and fry the garlic and onion for a minute.

2 Add in the prawn heads, stir-fry until the heads turn pink and cook till lightly browned and fragrant. Pour in the water and add in the chicken carcasses (cleaned and excess fat removed).

3 Bring to a boil, lower heat and simmer for 45 mins.

Noodles and Garnishes

4 Clean and devein the prawns (remove heads and keep the prawn heads in the freezer for another use). Bring a pot of water to the boil. Put the prawns in to cook. When they float on top (4 mins) remove and plunge them in cold water. Peel the shells off the prawns, halve horizontally along the vein, and set aside.

5 Cut the fish cake into slices and set aside. Peel the eggs, cut into halves and set aside.

6 Strain the soup base stock into a clean pot. Discard the prawn heads and chicken bones. Increase the heat to medium-high. Cook the pork or chicken in the stock for 10 mins or until just cooked. Remove and cool. Slice into thin slices. Keep the stock warm on a low heat.

7 Wash the bean sprouts. Drain and set aside. Wash the kang kong, remove the woody ends and snap the stems into 5 cm (2") lengths. Drain and set aside.

8 Bring a large pot of water to the boil. Blanch the bean sprouts and the kang kong separately. Set aside.

9 For each person, put some yellow noodles and rice vermicelli in a noodle strainer basket and cook for 50 secs until soft. Drain off the water. Put the noodles into a large noodle bowl with some bean sprouts at the bottom.

10 Top with some kang kong, prawns, pork or chicken meat, fish cake and half an egg.

11 Scoop some hot soup / stock on top. Garnish with crispy shallots and chilli paste (if desired).

Chilli Paste

1 Blend the chillies, onions, shrimps and garlic in a food processor, or pound in a mortar and pestle, to a rough paste.

2 Heat the oil and fry the spices on low heat until aromatic and the oil starts to separate.

3 Add the sugar and salt, mix in and cool.

Assam Laksa ~ Hot *and* Sour Fish Laksa

SERVES 6

800 g (1 lb 12 oz) fresh fish, e.g. mackerel, yellowtail

100 g (3½ oz) tamarind pulp

2 cups (500 mL) water (for the tamarind)

8 cups (2 litres) water (for the stock)

4–5 pieces dried tamarind peel (skin)

4 stalks laksa leaf / Vietnamese mint

1 packet dried Vietnamese rice noodles (bun hue)

Spice Paste

5 fresh red chillies, deseeded, chopped (less, if you prefer)

5 dried red chillies, deseeded and soaked, chopped

1 onion, or 200 g (7 oz) shallots (eschalots), chopped

30 g (1 oz) belachan (dried shrimp paste), toasted*

3 stalks lemongrass, white part only, chopped

1 Tbsp salt, or to taste

2 Tbsp sugar, or to taste

Toppings

1 cucumber, julienned

¼ piece fresh pineapple, diced, or 1 can tinned pineapple pieces, drained (juice reserved for stock)

1 red onion, thinly sliced

3–4 iceberg lettuce leaves, sliced 1 cm (⅜") wide

1 ginger flower, sliced fine (if available)

2 Tbsp thick prawn paste (har go), blended together with 50–100 mL (2–3 fl oz) water

1 lime, cut into wedges

1 cup mint leaves

1 fresh red chilli, sliced

This noodle soup dish has a complex and deeply satisfying flavour. It may not be as popular as its better-known cousin, curry laksa, but it still packs a punch. It's not an everyday food, but is certainly a dish that you yearn for, every now and then. Every so often, when I make 'Assam Laksa', the whole family come home to eat.

1 Gut and clean the fish. Place in a shallow dish for steaming. Steam the fish till cooked. Cool, then flake the flesh. Set aside. Strain the fish stock into a stock pot for the laksa.

2 Blend the spice paste ingredients in a food processor till fine.

3 Mix the tamarind pulp with 2 cups of water. Loosen with a fork. Leave to soak for a few minutes.

4 Add 8 cups of water to the fish stock in the stock pot. Put in the tamarind peels, laksa leaves, blended spice paste and strain the tamarind liquid in (discard the tamarind pulp). Add the reserved pineapple juice in, if using tinned pineapple.

5 Bring the laksa stock to a boil. Reduce the heat and simmer until aromatic. Add the flaked fish. Season with salt and sugar to taste. Keep warm.

Tip: If you wish, add a tin of 'sardines in tomato sauce' to the stock, for extra flavour.

6 Cook the rice noodles in boiling water. Rinse in cold water. Drain.

7 To serve, place a serving of noodles in individual noodle bowls. Top each bowl with a little of each of the topping ingredients.

8 Ladle very hot soup along with some fish over the bowl of noodles. Serve with some prawn paste, a wedge of lime, mint and chillies.

*See 'Basics' on page 167 for how to prepare toasted belachan. Alternatively, some Asian supermarkets stock pre-toasted belachan (e.g. Jeeny's brand).

When I was young, roaming hawkers selling 'Assam Laksa' would come to my street and stay for an hour or so. If you lived two stories up and didn't feel like running down to them, you could put your bowl and some money in a basket and dangle it through the window, down to the hawker. They would cook your noodles for you, place your bowl in the basket and you would raise it up. It was such fun!

Ching Tong Ngau Larm
~ Beef Broth Noodle Soup

A humble, warming beef noodle soup. Every region has its own variation.

SERVES 4

Spice Bag

1 piece cassia bark, or small cinnamon quill
3 star anise
4 cloves
1 tsp black peppercorns
1 tsp fennel seeds
2 tsp coriander seeds

2 chicken carcasses (chicken frames)
1 kg (2 lb 3 oz) beef brisket
2 litres (8 cups) water
1 brown onion
1 bunch coriander (cilantro), roots and stems (reserve the leaves section for serving)
4 slices ginger, cut 1 cm (⅜") thick

To Serve

1 daikon (white radish)
1 Tbsp sugar
3 tsp salt
1 Tbsp fish sauce
8 beef balls with tendons, halved
1 kg (2 lb 3 oz) hor fun (flat rice noodles), sliced
Coriander (cilantro) leaves (reserved)
1 fresh red chilli, sliced (optional)

1 Prepare the soup stock the day before. Lightly roast the spices and put them in a muslin bag. Tie securely.

2 Wash and clean the chicken carcasses, remove the fatty skins.

3 Bring a large saucepan of water to the boil. Put in the chicken carcasses and the whole piece of beef brisket. Parboil for 15–20 mins. Remove from heat and discard the water. Rinse the chicken bones and the brisket with clean water.

4 Fill a large stockpot with 2 litres (8 cups) of water. Put in the chicken bones, beef brisket, onion, coriander roots and stems, ginger and the spice bag. Bring to the boil, then lower heat to a vigorous simmer / gentle boil for 1½ hrs, or until the beef is tender but not falling apart. Remove the beef onto a plate or container to cool. Strain the soup stock. Discard the chicken bones, onion and spices. Cool the stock and refrigerate.

5 The next day, remove the fat from the top of the soup stock. Pour the stock into a large pot to heat up. Peel and cut the daikon into chunks and cook in the stock until tender.

6 Half an hour before serving, put the beef brisket back in the soup stock to warm up. Add the sugar, salt and fish sauce to the stock. Taste and adjust seasoning. Add in the beef balls. Remove the beef brisket and cut into thick slices.

7 Blanch the hor fun in boiling water. Drain and divide the noodles among 4 bowls. Top each bowl with beef brisket, beef tendon balls, daikon and hot soup. Garnish with coriander leaves and freshly cut chilli, if desired.

Note: Start this recipe the day before.

Shared Dishes

Hung Siu Ngau Yook
~ Braised Beef Shin *with* Soya Eggs

This recipe is simple to make but requires a bit of forward planning. To get the most out of beef shin, it's best to cook it slowly over a low heat. So, it's a good idea to prepare the beef and eggs ahead of time. They can be kept in the fridge until you're ready to serve.

SERVES 4–6

1 kg – 1.5 kg (2 lb 3 oz – 3 lb 5 oz) beef shin

Master Sauce
(see See Yau Gai ~ Soya Sauce Chicken recipe on page 87)

6 eggs

Pickled daikon and carrot, to serve (optional)

1   If your beef shin is very wide / thick, get your butcher to cut it lengthwise into 2 pieces of about 10 cm (4") diameter. Wash and trim fat off if necessary.

2   Bring the master sauce to the boil in a large pot. Put the beef shin pieces in the master sauce. Bring it back to the boil. Cover. Turn heat to low and simmer for 2 hours. Cook till meat is tender. Test for tenderness with a metal skewer. The skewer should go through easily.

3   Remove meat, cool, cling wrap and refrigerate overnight. It's easier to slice when cold.

4   To make the soya eggs, steam or boil the eggs — 7 mins for soft centred yolks, 10 mins for hard yolks. Put the eggs in cold water straight away. Peel the eggs and place in the cooled master sauce to marinate overnight.

5   To serve, slice the beef into thin slices and arrange on a plate. Reheat briefly in microwave. Serve warm with some of the braising liquid, the halved soya eggs and some pickles, if desired.

See Yau Gai ~ Soya Sauce Chicken

Often seen hanging in Chinese BBQ shop windows or served in Chinese restaurants, this dish can also be made at home. Reserve the master sauce after cooking and it can be used to make another chicken or other dishes.

SERVES 4

1.3 kg – 1.5 kg (2 lb 14 oz – 3 lb 5 oz) whole chicken, or chicken marylands

Master Sauce

1 Tbsp oil

3 green shallots (green onions / scallions), white part only

1 thumb-size piece ginger, smashed or sliced

6 cloves

2–3 star anise

1 cinnamon quill

1½ cups all-purpose soy sauce (e.g. Kikkoman brand)

2 Tbsp dark soy sauce

½ cup Shaoxing wine, or cooking wine

40 g (1⅜ oz) rock sugar, or 50 g (1¾ oz) brown sugar

1½ cups water

2 tsp sesame oil (rub for chicken)

1 Clean the chicken well, inside the cavity and skin. Pat dry with paper towel.

2 In a deep pot, add the oil, white parts of the shallots, ginger, cloves, star anise and cinnamon quill. Fry over low heat until fragrant and the shallots and ginger are lightly browned. Add in the soy, dark soy, wine, sugar and water. Increase heat to high and bring to a boil.

3 Put the whole chicken in, breasts down first. Bring the sauce back to the boil, then reduce the heat to a low simmer. Cover and cook on low heat for 45 mins, turning the chicken every 15 mins. Turn the heat off. Test the thigh meat with a skewer. If no pink liquid oozes out, the meat is cooked. If pink liquid does come out, leave it in the sauce for 10–15 mins more.

Note: If using marylands, submerge them in the sauce. Bring the sauce back to the boil, cook on a low simmer for 20 mins. Turn the heat off and leave it in the soy sauce for 20 mins, covered.

4 Drain the chicken and place on a plate to cool.

5 Rub sesame oil on the chicken. Cut the chicken into bite-sized pieces and serve with a bit of sauce on the side or on top.

Note: When the sauce has cooled, transfer to a container and keep as a 'master sauce' in the fridge or freezer for another chicken or other braised soya dishes, e.g. shin beef, soya eggs (see page 85). Replenish the sauce after 2 uses with fresh spices and add extra soy, wine, sugar and boiled water. Discard the old (used) spices. The 'master sauce' can keep indefinitely in the freezer.

Cha Siew ~ Chinese BBQ Pork

This home-made 'cha siew' is easy to make and tastes just as good as those glistening red strips of meat you might have seen hanging in the windows of Chinese BBQ shops. This recipe could be cooked in the oven or on the BBQ.

SERVES 6–8

1 kg – 1.2 kg (2 lb 3 oz – 2 lb 10 oz) pork neck, or pork shoulder*

Marinade

2 Tbsp brown sugar
¼ cup honey or maltose
¼ cup hoisin sauce
2 Tbsp soy sauce
2 Tbsp Shaoxing wine, or cooking wine
1 tsp 5-spice powder^
1 Tbsp garlic powder
1 Tbsp oil
1 Tbsp Worcestershire sauce
½ tsp salt
2 Tbsp extra honey

*For a more juicy, moist and tender texture use pork belly. For a leaner version, use pork loin or pork shoulder.

^See 'Basics' on page 166 for how to make your own 5-spice powder.

1. Cut the pork lengthwise about 2.5–4 cm (1–1½") thick.

2. Mix the marinade ingredients together in a bowl. Coat the pork pieces in the marinade. Put the pork and the marinade in a glass container or zip-lock bag and refrigerate overnight, or 4 hours minimum.

To Roast Pork

1. Remove the pork pieces from the fridge 1 hour before cooking.

2. Preheat oven to 180°C (360°F). Line a roasting pan with foil. Place a rack on top.

3. Remove the pork from the marinade and place on the rack. Reserve the marinade. Add ½ cup water to the bottom of the roasting pan to create steam.

4. Put the reserved marinade into a small saucepan. Add in the extra honey and simmer till syrupy. Remove from heat.

5. Brush the pork pieces with the marinade and roast for 15 mins; turn and baste again with marinade, roast for another 15 mins; turn and baste both sides again and roast for a further 10 mins.

6. Turn oven to grill mode at 200–220°C (390–430°F) and grill until the pork is slightly charred and glossy. Turn the pork over and grill the other side, basting with the marinade, until caramelised (10–15 mins). Remove from oven and rest. Brush the marinade on both sides of the pork while still hot. (Total cooking time 50–55 mins).

7. Slice into pieces and serve with some greens on a bed of rice, or as a shared dish, or serve alongside crispy pork (siu yook, see page 91) as a starter.

Tips:
Start this recipe the day before for a deeper flavour.
Leftover cha siew could be diced and used in fried rice.

Siu Yook ~ Crispy Pork Belly

SERVES 4

1 kg (2 lb 3 oz) piece belly pork

1½ Tbsp Shaoxing wine, or cooking wine

1 tsp 5-spice powder*

2 tsp salt

¾ tsp white pepper

¼ tsp bicarbonate of soda

1 Tbsp vinegar

200 g (7 oz) rock salt or coarse salt

*See 'Basics' on page 166 for how to make your own 5-spice powder.

1. Clean the pork, pat it dry with paper towel. Using a metal skewer, prick lots and lots of holes in the skin only.

2. Turn the pork over, rub the flesh with the cooking wine.

3. Mix together the 5-spice powder, salt and pepper. Rub it evenly all over the flesh. Turn the pork right side up and place it on a plate or container. Dry the skin with paper towel and place it in the fridge to dry, uncovered, for 12 hours or overnight.

4. Remove the pork from the fridge 1 hour before roasting.

5. Position a rack on the middle rung of the oven. Preheat oven to 180°C (360°F).

6. Place the pork on a large piece of foil. Fold up the sides around the pork to enclose it, leaving a 2 cm (¾") allowance above the top (skin) of the pork (to hold the salt in).

7. Transfer the pork to a baking tray. Dry the skin with paper towel if there is any moisture.

8. Mix the bicarb soda with the vinegar. Brush the skin with the vinegar solution. Then place the rock salt on the skin, pressing it in lightly. (The foil will prevent it falling down the sides).

9. Put the pork in the preheated oven to roast for 1 hour.

10. Remove the pork and transfer it to your benchtop.

11. Move the rack to the bottom rung of the oven, about 25 cm (10") from the heat source. Switch the oven to grill mode on high (240°C / 460°F).

12. Unfold the foil and scrape the salt off the top and sides of the pork. Pat the skin dry with paper towel. Return the pork to the baking tray.

13. Place it under the grill for 30–35 mins, rotating the tray halfway through. Grill until the skin is golden, puffed up and bubbly. Watch that it does not get too brown.

14. Remove from oven, rest 10–15 mins.

15. Slice into 1.5–2 cm (¾") thick slices and then cut up into small bite-sized pieces. Serve as a shared dish.

An adaptation from Recipe Tin Eats (Nagi Maehashi)

Tip: Start this recipe the night before. Allow the skin to dry out in the fridge — 12 hours or overnight — for a crispier result.

Steamed Tofu *with* Prawn Paste

A popular dish to order for dinner when eating out in restaurants. It is prized for its light taste and texture. Only the best quality, freshest ingredients can be used in such a lightly-seasoned dish.

MAKES 12 PIECES

6 squares of tofu, silken or regular (e.g. Evergreen brand)

120 g (4¼ oz) fresh prawn meat, washed and drained

¼ tsp salt

Pinch of white pepper

⅛ tsp sugar

½ tsp sesame oil

1 tsp egg white, lightly whisked

1 green shallot (green onion / scallion), chopped, to garnish

Soy Dressing

1 tsp dark soy sauce

2 tsp light soy sauce

¾ tsp caster sugar (superfine sugar)

1 Tbsp water

1 Tbsp cooking oil

1 Cut the prawns into pieces and then pound in a mortar and pestle until mince-like.

2 Place in a mixing bowl. Season with salt, pepper, sugar, sesame oil and egg white. Mix and stir the prawn mixture around in one direction until the mixture is springy and gluey. Place in the fridge if not using straight away.

3 Cut the 6 squares of tofu into rectangular halves. Using a teaspoon, carefully scoop out a small amount of tofu 0.5 cm (¼") deep, from the top of each rectangular piece, leaving a border around it. Stuff each piece with a portion of prawn filling.

4 Arrange the stuffed tofu on a heatproof plate, leaving space between each. Steam for about 6–8 mins over simmering water until prawns are opaque.

5 Meanwhile, stir the soy dressing ingredients together in a bowl. Warm it up slightly in the microwave or on the stove.

6 Remove tofu from heat. Spoon the soy dressing over the steamed tofu and garnish with chopped green shallots.

Tip: It is important to mix the prawns sufficiently to get the right springy texture.

Jee Yook Jing Daan
~ Steamed Silken Egg
with Pork Mince

This home-style dish has been enjoyed in our family for generations. It is a favourite of my grandchildren who often request that I make it for dinner. It's simple, nutritious and tasty. The creaminess of the egg blends in well with steamed rice.

SERVES 4

- 200 g (7 oz) lean pork mince
- ¼ tsp salt
- ¼ tsp sugar
- 2 tsp cooking oil
- Dash of sesame oil
- 2 eggs
- 120 mL (4 fl oz) water
- ¼ tsp chicken stock powder
- 2 tsp soy sauce, to serve
- 1 green shallot (green onion/scallion), chopped, to garnish (optional)

1 Season the pork mince with the salt, sugar and oils.

2 Beat the eggs, add the water and chicken powder. Pour the egg mixture onto the seasoned pork. Stir briefly to mix together.

3 Transfer the pork and egg mixture to a deep round heatproof plate, using the back of a fork to spread the meat out evenly. Place over boiling water in a steamer or on a steaming rack in a wok or large pan. Steam for 10 mins on medium heat. Lower the heat and steam for a further 10 mins.

Tip: Lowering the heat halfway through cooking will prevent the eggs from overcooking.

4 Just before serving, drizzle with soy sauce and garnish with green shallots. Serve with steamed rice or as a shared dish.

....

Variations:

Substitute the pork mince with chicken mince, cha siew (BBQ pork) or diced ham (omit added seasonings), if preferred.

If using cha siew or ham, shorten the cooking time.

Add some frozen green peas or corn kernels in before steaming.

Jing Yook Beng ~ Steamed Pork Rissole *with* Water Chestnuts

SERVES 4

3 dried shiitake mushrooms (dong gu)

40 g (1⅜ oz) dried cloud ear fungus strips (wan yee)

30 g (1 oz) water chestnuts (maa tai)

300 g (10½ oz) pork mince

½ tsp salt

Dash of white pepper

½ tsp sugar

½ tsp chicken stock powder

2 tsp cornflour (cornstarch)

1 Tbsp oil

50 mL (1¾ fl oz) water

1 green shallot (green onion / scallion), chopped, to garnish (optional)

1 Soak the dried shiitake mushrooms and cloud ear fungus until soft, remove hard stems, then dice the mushrooms and chop the cloud ear fungus. Set aside.

2 Chop the water chestnuts. Set aside.

3 Marinate the minced pork with the salt, pepper, sugar, chicken powder, cornflour, oil and water. Mix in well with a fork or chopsticks until the mixture is a bit sticky. Add the mushrooms, cloud ear fungus and water chestnuts to the pork mixture. Stir in to combine.

4 Transfer the mixture onto a deep heatproof plate.

5 Place on a steaming rack in a wok or large pan and steam on high for 10–15 mins.

6 Garnish with green shallots. Serve with steamed rice or as a shared dish.

Variations:

Pork Rissole with Salted Fish (Haam Yu)

Pork Rissole with Preserved Vegetables (Mui Choy)

Pork Rissole with Preserved Mustard Leaves (Tung Choy)

Pork Rissole with Mushrooms & Chinese Sausage (Dong Gu & Larp Cheong)

Pork Rissole with Dried Squid (Diu Pin)

You can try out different flavours of pork rissole by replacing the mushrooms, cloud ear fungus and water chestnuts with the variations listed here.

The replacement ingredient will need to be prepared first, e.g. soaked, washed, chopped or diced.

If the replacement ingredient is very salty, soak well to wash off most of the salt and omit the ½ tsp salt in the pork marinade.

Picture features Nanna Brab's silver spoon

This rustic home-style dish has been a favourite with children and adults alike for generations. The pork is steamed to keep it tender and juicy. The water chestnuts provide a bit of crunch and sweetness. It can be made in many different variations.

Mapo Tofu ~ Grandma's Tofu

This is a traditional Chinese home-cooked family dish that is very comforting. The spiciness level can be adjusted to your liking.

SERVES 4

450 g (1 lb) regular tofu

2 shiitake mushrooms, fresh or dried (soaked)

2 Tbsp oil

300 g (10½ oz) pork mince

2 tsp garlic, minced

2 tsp ginger, minced (optional)

1 cup (about 3 stalks) green shallots (green onions / scallions), white and green parts separated, chopped

2 tsp cooking wine or sake

1 cup chicken stock* or water

Sugar, to taste

1 tsp cornflour (cornstarch), mixed with 2 Tbsp water

½ tsp sesame oil

Bean Sauce Mixture

1½ Tbsp miso paste, or dou ban jiang (Chinese brown bean paste)

1 tsp chilli bean paste (optional)

1 Tbsp soy sauce

2 tsp hoisin sauce

1   Mix the bean sauce ingredients together in a bowl. Set aside.

2   Drain the tofu, cut into cubes. Set aside. Dice the mushrooms. Set aside.

3   Heat 2 Tbsp oil in a pan or wok over medium-high heat. Stir-fry the pork mince, breaking up the lumps and cook until it changes colour.

4   Add into the mince the mushrooms, garlic, ginger and white parts of the shallots. Mix in and cook for 1 min. Then add the cooking wine.

5   Add in the bean sauce mixture and the chicken stock or water. Stir, increase heat to bring to a boil.

6   Add the tofu cubes, gently mix in and cook until it boils again. Lower heat and cook for 2–3 mins. Season to taste with the sugar.

7   Thicken the sauce with the cornflour and water mixture. Mix in the green parts of the shallots and do a quick stir. Add the sesame oil. Dish up. Serve as a shared dish with steamed rice.

*See 'Basics' on page 167 for how to make homemade chicken stock.

Steamed Chicken *with* Mushrooms

A child-friendly, home-cooked family dish. Steaming the chicken keeps it juicy and tender.

SERVES 4

- 600 g (1 lb 5 oz) chicken, bone-in*
- 1 small knob ginger, sliced
- 1 tsp salt
- ½ tsp sugar
- Dash of pepper
- 2 tsp sesame oil
- 1 Tbsp oil
- 1 Tbsp Shaoxing wine, or cooking wine
- 1 Tbsp cornflour (cornstarch)
- 2 dried shiitake mushrooms, soaked
- 8 g (¼ oz) cloud ear fungus (wan yee), soaked
- 15 pieces lily buds / golden needles (kum jum), soaked
- 2 green shallots (green onions / scallions), divided (white part cut into 2 cm (¾") lengths, green part reserved for garnish)

1 Cut the chicken into small pieces. Marinate with the ginger, salt, sugar, pepper, oils, wine and cornflour. Set aside for 15 mins.

2 Rinse and squeeze the water out of the mushrooms. Slice into pieces.

3 Cut off the hard stems from the cloud ear fungus.

4 Wash and rinse the lily buds, then squeeze dry. Tie a knot in each.

5 Add the sliced mushrooms, cloud ear fungus, lily buds and the white parts of the shallots to the marinated chicken. Mix into the chicken.

6 Tip the contents into a rimmed glass plate or pie dish. Spread out evenly and steam in a wok on high heat for 20–25 mins. Stir the contents to check if the chicken pieces are cooked. Remove from heat, garnish with the reserved green parts of the shallots.

7 Serve as a shared main with rice and some steamed Asian greens.

*Bone-in chicken can be substituted with thigh fillets if preferred.

Stewed Chicken *with* Mushrooms *and* Potatoes

This family-friendly stew is popular with kids and adults due to its tender chicken and vegetables that soak up the caramel-like sauce.

SERVES 4

1 kg – 1.3 kg (2 lb 3 oz – 2 lb 14 oz) whole chicken*, bone-in

½ tsp salt

6–8 dried shiitake mushrooms, soaked

2 medium potatoes, peeled

2 Tbsp cooking oil

4 slices ginger

1 clove garlic, crushed

2 Tbsp light soy sauce

1 Tbsp dark soy sauce

2 tsp sugar

1 Tbsp oyster sauce

1½ cups water

1 Tbsp cornflour (cornstarch), mixed with ½ cup water

2 tsp sesame oil

1 Cut the chicken into bite-sized pieces. Sprinkle with ½ tsp salt.

2 Remove the stalks from the mushrooms, cut into halves. Cut the potatoes into quarters.

3 Heat the cooking oil, fry the ginger and garlic for 30 secs. Add in the chicken pieces, mushrooms and potatoes. Stir-fry for 1–2 mins.

4 Add the light and dark soy sauces, sugar, oyster sauce and water. Bring to the boil, lower the heat and simmer for 30 mins.

5 Thicken the sauce with the cornflour mixture. Simmer for another 1–2 mins. Add in the sesame oil. Serve hot as a shared dish with steamed white rice.

*You may prefer to substitute the whole chicken with chicken pieces. e.g. maryland, thighs.

Picture features Eddie's Chinese teapot (1968)

SHARED DISHES

Braised Belly Pork Ribs *with* Eggs

SERVES 4

2 Tbsp oil
4–5 slices ginger
500 g (1 lb 2 oz) belly pork ribs, cut into 5 cm (2") pieces
4 cloves garlic, peeled
4 cups (1 litre) water
1½ Tbsp rice wine vinegar
1½ Tbsp dark soy sauce
3 Tbsp light soy sauce
4 star anise
100 g (3½ oz) rock sugar
4 hard-boiled eggs

1   Heat the oil and ginger in a saucepan or clay pot. Add in the pork ribs and garlic and stir-fry for 3–5 mins.

2   Add the water and bring it to the boil. Remove any impurities that float on the top. Then add in the vinegar, dark soy, light soy, star anise and rock sugar. Return to the boil, then lower the heat to a slow boil and braise the pork for 1½ – 2 hours. Stir occasionally.

3   When the pork is almost tender, add in the hard-boiled eggs and continue to cook until the pork is meltingly tender. Taste and adjust seasoning. Serve hot with steamed rice.

Mun Ngau Larm
~ Beef Stew *with* Daikon *and* Carrots

A traditional Cantonese home-cooked dish. This dish tastes much better if left overnight for the flavours to develop.

SERVES 4

1 kg (2 lb 3 oz) chuck steak, or beef brisket, cut into 2.5 cm (1") pieces

2 Tbsp cooking oil

1 thumb-size piece ginger, sliced

3 green shallots (green onions / scallions), white part, cut into 2–3 sections

3 cloves garlic, crushed

¼ cup Shaoxing wine, or cooking wine

2–3 dried long red chillies

4 bay leaves

3 star anise

1 piece cassia bark, or small cinnamon quill

1 tsp black peppercorns

8 cloves

5 cups (1.25 litres) water

¼ cup light soy sauce

2 Tbsp dark soy sauce

2 Tbsp miso paste, or brown bean sauce

2 Tbsp hoisin sauce

20 g (¾ oz) rock sugar

Extra water, if needed

2 carrots, peeled, cut into chunks

500 g (1 lb 2 oz) daikon (white radish), peeled, cut into chunks

Salt, to taste

1 green shallot, chopped diagonally, to garnish

1 Blanch the beef pieces in boiling water for 10 mins. Drain.

2 Heat the oil in a large saucepan. Fry the ginger, white parts of the shallots and the garlic. Add the beef and fry for a few minutes. Add the wine, chillies, bay leaves, star anise, cassia bark, peppercorns, cloves and 5 cups of water to cover the beef. Bring to a boil, reduce to medium heat and simmer, covered, for 40–50 mins.

3 Then add the light and dark soy sauces, miso paste, hoisin and rock sugar. Continue to simmer, uncovered, for 1–1½ hours. Add more water if needed.

4 Test the beef to see if it's tender, but not meltingly tender. Put in the carrots and daikon and cook for 30 mins or until the vegetables are tender. Season to taste.

5 Garnish with green shallots. Serve as a shared main with rice or noodles.

Mui Choy Kau Yoke
~ Belly Pork *with* Preserved Vegetable

SERVES 4–6

1 packet mui choy (preserved vegetable / preserved mustard greens)

500 g – 800 g (1 lb 2 oz – 1 lb 12 oz) piece belly pork

3–4 Tbsp dark soy sauce

3 cloves garlic, peeled

1 x 2.5 cm (1") piece fresh ginger, sliced into 4–5 slices

4 star anise

1 cinnamon quill

3 cups (750 mL) chicken stock* or water

1 piece (50 g, 1¾ oz) brown slab sugar, or white sugar

1 Tbsp oyster sauce

Soy sauce, to taste

Sugar, to taste

1 green shallot (green onion / scallion), chopped, to garnish

Tip: Soak the preserved vegetable the night before.

*See 'Basics' on page 167 for how to make homemade chicken stock.

1 Soak the mui choy in water overnight to rehydrate it and to remove the salt from the vegetable.

2 The next day, rinse twice to clean the mui choy of sand and grit. Squeeze dry and cut into 0.5 cm (¼") pieces. Set aside.

3 Fill a pot with 1 litre (4 cups) of water. Bring to the boil. Place the piece of pork in the water and vigorous simmer / gentle boil for 30 mins. Remove, cool for a few minutes, then rub the dark soy sauce all over the skin of the pork. Set aside to air dry.

4 Meanwhile, dry fry the mui choy in a clay pot or cast iron pot. Add the garlic and ginger, stir the mui choy, moving it around so that it does not burn at the bottom. Turn off the heat.

5 When the pork is cool enough to handle, cut into 0.5 cm x 5 cm (¼" x 2") pieces and place neatly on top of the mui choy in the pot.

Note: For a restaurant look, the piece of pork could be deep fried to give the skin a 'blistered' and brown look. Cool, then slice into 0.5 cm x 5 cm (¼" x 2") pieces. Lay neatly on top of the mui choy in the pot.

6 Put in the star anise, cinnamon, stock or water, slab sugar and oyster sauce and bring it to a boil. Simmer for 40 mins or until the pork pieces are tender. Add more stock or water if needed. Season to taste with soy and sugar.

7 Garnish with green shallots. Serve directly in the clay pot or cast iron pot as a shared main. Serve with rice.

Steamed Whole Fish *with* Ginger *and* Shallots

A dish to be shared among many, whether it's at home for a weeknight family dinner or as one of the courses at a Chinese banquet.

SERVES 4

500 g – 600 g (1 lb 2 oz – 1 lb 5 oz) fresh whole fish e.g. bream, flounder, snapper

Salt and pepper

1 thumb-size piece ginger, finely sliced and julienned

2 green shallots (green onions / scallions), finely sliced diagonally

3 stalks coriander (cilantro), cut into 4–5 cm (1½"–2") lengths

½ cup (125 mL) oil

1 fresh long red chilli, sliced diagonally, to garnish (optional)

Soy Dressing

¼ cup (60 mL) light soy sauce

1 Tbsp Shaoxing wine, or cooking wine

1 Tbsp hot water

1 tsp sugar

1 Clean and gut the fish. Drain and pat dry. Make 2 slits on both sides of the fish body. Season with salt and pepper.

2 Place the fish on a long, large heatproof plate. Place the ginger on top of the fish and some in the stomach opening.

3 Steam the fish over boiling water on a rack in the wok for 8–10 mins. Test at 8 mins to see if the flesh comes away from the bone at the thickest part. If it does, it's done. Turn off the heat.

4 While the fish is steaming, mix the soy dressing ingredients together.

5 When the fish is cooked, pour off the cloudy liquid from the fish. Spread the sliced green shallots and coriander over the fish.

6 Heat up the oil to a high point. Then pour it directly over the shallots and coriander.

7 Drizzle the soy dressing over the fish. Serve while it's hot. Garnish with chilli if desired. Serve as a shared main.

Variation:

If using a fish fillet instead of a whole fish, the cooking time will be shortened. Clean and pat dry the fish fillet. Put on a heatproof plate. Place some julienned ginger on top. Steam for 5–7 mins, depending on the thickness of the fillet. Test if it's cooked. Pour over the hot oil and garnish with shallots, coriander and soy dressing, as for the whole fish.

Facing page features a deep fish dish from Jeanie's father (1970s)

Yong Tau Foo ~ Tofu *and* Vegetables Stuffed *with* Fish Paste

SERVES 4

500 g (1 lb 2 oz) fresh red fish fillets, mackerel or sea perch fillets
2 tsp (10 g) salt, dissolved in 200 mL (6¾ fl oz) ice water
1 Tbsp cornflour (cornstarch)
¾ tsp sugar
½ tsp baking powder
½ tsp white pepper
1 egg white
Extra ice water
1 Tbsp cooking oil

Vegetable Components
1 small red capsicum (pepper)
1 bitter melon (bitter gourd)
1 small eggplant (aubergine)
2 pieces tau foo pok (fried tofu puffs)
2 long chillies, red or green

Black Bean Sauce
1 Tbsp oil
1 clove garlic, minced
1 tsp ginger, minced
2 Tbsp black bean sauce
2 tsp sugar
1 cup water or stock
1 tsp cornflour (cornstarch), mixed with 1 Tbsp water
1 fresh red chilli, sliced, as garnish

1. Clean and pin bone (if any) the fish fillets. Cut the fillets into small chunks. Set aside to drain.

2. Dissolve the salt in the ice water.

3. Blend the fish in a food processor for 1 min, or until fine. Remove and transfer to a large mixing bowl. Then add in the cornflour, sugar, baking powder, white pepper, egg white and half of the salt water. Mix until well combined. Add the remaining salt water a bit at a time. The fish texture should be firm and elastic, but not hard. Add a bit of extra ice water if needed.

4. Wet your hand and scoop the fish paste up and pound it against the bowl until it becomes springy. Pound about 30 times. Extra pounding gives a more springy texture.

5. Rinse a bowl or container with water. Place the fish paste in it, cover and refrigerate until ready to use.

6. Prepare the yong tau foo components:
   Capsicum — quarter them and discard seeds
   Bitter melon — cut into 2 cm (¾") rings, remove seeds and white core
   Eggplant — slice into 2 cm (¾") thick rounds and make a deep slit in the middle of each, about ¾ of the way through
   Tau foo pok — halve them and remove a bit of the tofu inside
   Chillies — make a slit on one side lengthwise and remove seeds.

7. Stuff the fish paste into the capsicum, bitter melon, eggplant, tau foo pok and chillies using a butter knife. Smooth the fish paste with a bit of water on the surface.

8. Heat up 1 Tbsp cooking oil in a pan on medium heat. Panfry the yong tau foo pieces, making sure the fish is cooked and the vegetables are lightly browned. Set aside.

9. For the sauce, heat 1 Tbsp oil in a pan on low heat. Fry the ginger and garlic until lightly browned, add in the black bean sauce, sugar and water. Stir well and bring to a boil. Season to taste. Thicken the sauce with the cornflour and water mixture. Add in the sliced chilli.

10. To serve: spoon the sauce over the yong tau foo; or serve it as a dipping sauce; or mix the stuffed vegetables in the sauce and lightly toss, then dish up and serve.

Braised Tofu *with* Shiitake Mushrooms

Try to find good quality shiitake mushrooms for this dish, allowing them ample time to plump up in water before cooking. The flavour burst from the mushrooms is complemented well by the fresh tofu and crisp snow peas. You can replace the oyster sauce with mushroom soy sauce to make this dish suitable for vegetarians.

SERVES 4

1 packet (900 g, 2 lb) firm white tofu (12 pieces)

1 cup oil, for frying

8 dried shiitake mushrooms, rinsed and rehydrated in water until soft

12 snow peas or other greens e.g. sugar snap peas

1½ Tbsp oil

1 tsp minced ginger or 3–4 slices ginger

2 green shallots (green onions / scallions), white part only, cut into 5 cm (2") lengths

2 tsp soy sauce

1 Tbsp oyster sauce

1 tsp dark soy sauce

1 cup water

2 tsp cornflour (cornstarch), mixed with 3 Tbsp water

Dash of sesame oil

1 Cut 8 pieces of tofu into halves. Pat dry with paper towel.

2 Heat up 1 cup of oil in a saucepan. Deep fry the tofu pieces, in 3 batches until light brown. Drain on paper towel and set aside.

3 Drain the shiitake mushrooms, squeeze the water out. Reserve the mushroom water. String the snow peas.

4 Heat 1½ Tbsp oil in a wok or clay pot. Stir-fry the snow peas in the oil for a few seconds. Remove and set aside. Add in the ginger, white parts of the shallots and mushrooms. Stir and cook for 2–3 mins. Add in the sauces, water and the reserved mushroom water. Put in the fried tofu pieces and let the sauce come to a boil. Reduce the heat, put the lid on and simmer for 20 mins, turning the tofu mixture once. If the liquid evaporates too quickly, add some water.

5 Adjust to taste, adding more soy sauce or oyster sauce, as needed. Thicken the sauce with the cornflour mixture. Put the snow peas in and toss them lightly into the dish. Add a dash of sesame oil. Dish up and serve with steamed rice as a shared main.

 To make it a vegetarian dish, simply replace the oyster sauce with mushroom soy sauce.

New Year Jai ~ Buddha's Delight ⓥ

This is a very popular dish with Chinese families for Chinese New Year. Make it the night before to let the flavours develop. Devout Buddhists will eat 'jai' only for the whole day. This dish is vegetarian.

SERVES 4–5

Dried Items

5 dried shiitake mushrooms

60 g (2⅛ oz) lily buds / golden needles (kum jum)

8 g (¼ oz) cloud ear fungus (wan yee)

8 pitted red dates (hung zou) (or remove pits after soaking)

8 soybean knots, or bean curd sticks

1 packet (100 g, 3½ oz) bean vermicelli (fun see) (e.g. Long Kow (Double Phoenix) brand)

5 g (⅛ oz) black moss (fatt choy)

2 tsp oil

Fresh Items

10 wombok leaves (Chinese cabbage)

8 snow peas

6 baby corn

½ carrot

6 fried tofu puffs (tau foo pok)

3 cm (1⅛") piece ginger, sliced

4 Tbsp oil

4 pieces fermented white bean curd (foo yee) or red bean curd (lam yee), mashed

5 g (⅛ oz) rock sugar, or sugar

Salt, to taste

Tip: Cook this dish in advance to allow the flavours to develop.

1 Wash the dried mushrooms, soak them overnight. Remove the stalks and cut into halves if they're very large. Reserve the mushroom water. Soak the lily buds overnight, cut off the hard ends and tie each into a knot.

2 Soak the cloud ear fungus for 30 mins, remove the hard stalks. Soak the red dates for 30 mins, remove pits if not already pitted. Soak the soybean knots or bean curd sticks till soft. Soak the bean vermicelli for 30 mins. Soak the black moss in water with 2 tsp oil to remove any sand and grit. Drain all the soaked items and set aside.

3 Wash the wombok leaves, slice in half lengthwise and then cut into 4 cm (1½") pieces, crosswise. Wash and string the snow peas, wash the baby corn. Peel and slice the carrot. Cut the tofu puffs into halves. Set the fresh items aside.

4 Heat 4 Tbsp oil over medium-high heat in a large saucepan. Add the ginger and mushrooms, stir-fry for 1 min, then add the cloud ear fungus, lily buds and red dates and stir-fry for 30 secs. Then add the fermented white bean curd and stir the mixture into the ingredients. Add the reserved mushroom water, put the lid on and simmer for 3–5 mins.

5 Remove the lid and put in the wombok, tofu puffs, bean curd knots, carrots, baby corn, bean vermicelli, rock sugar and salt, to taste. Cook until the wombok is wilted. Add in the snow peas and black moss and cook for another minute.

6 Serve with a bit of black moss and 2 red dates on top, in individual bowls, or as a shared main.

Chicken Marsala Curry

A very flavoursome, light and fragrant curry made without the addition of coconut milk.

SERVES 4

Spice Mix

6 Tbsp (120 mL) cooking oil

1 cinnamon quill

2 star anise

8 cloves

6 green cardamom pods

½ tsp cumin seeds, toasted and ground

½ tsp fennel seeds, toasted and ground

1 brown onion, sliced

2 sprigs curry leaves (removed from centre stems)

8 cloves garlic, minced

40 g (1⅜ oz) ginger, minced

500 g (1 lb 2 oz) chicken pieces, bone-in, or chicken fillets

2 large potatoes, peeled, cut into chunks

2 tomatoes, quartered

5 Tbsp meat curry powder (less, if desired) (e.g. Babas or Ayam brands)

2 tsp salt, or to taste

2 cups (500 mL) water

20 g (¾ oz) cashews, ground in spice grinder and blended with 200 mL (6¾ fl oz) water to form a paste

1 Heat the oil in a pan. Sauté the spice mix ingredients in the oil until fragrant, about 3 mins.

2 Add the chicken, potatoes and tomatoes to the pan. Stir to coat in the spices. Cover with a lid. Cook for 3 mins.

3 Add in the curry powder, salt and water. Cook for a further 15 mins, covered.

4 Add in the cashew nut paste, lower the heat and cook for 3 mins.

5 Serve with steamed rice or roti.

Tip: The curry tastes even better if left overnight for the flavours to develop.

Nonya Curry Chicken

SERVES 4

Spice Paste

3 Tbsp coriander seeds

1 tsp cumin seeds

1 tsp fennel seeds

10 dried red chillies, soaked, deseeded, chopped into pieces

2 red onions, roughly chopped

3 cloves garlic, peeled

15 g (½ oz) belachan (dried shrimp paste), toasted*

15 g (½ oz) fresh turmeric, sliced

5 Tbsp cooking oil

1 star anise

2 cloves

1 cinnamon quill

6 sprigs curry leaves

1.3 kg – 1.5 kg (3 lb) chicken pieces

3 potatoes, peeled, cut into chunks

400 mL (13½ fl oz) coconut milk

100 mL (3⅜ fl oz) coconut cream

2 tsp salt, or to taste

1 tsp sugar, or to taste

1 For the spice paste, roast the coriander, cumin and fennel seeds in a frypan over low heat till lightly browned. Grind to a powder. Blend the chillies, onions, garlic, belachan and turmeric to make a paste. Add the roasted spice powders. Set aside.

2 Heat the oil in a large pot. Add the star anise, cloves, cinnamon quill and curry leaves (removed from the centre stems) and fry over low heat. Then add in the blended spice paste and fry slowly over low heat until fragrant. Add in 2–3 Tbsp coconut cream if it's too dry. Fry until the oil separates.

3 Add the chicken pieces, coating them in the spices. Add the potatoes and coconut milk. Put the lid on and cook over medium heat for 30 mins or until the chicken is tender.

4 Remove the lid, add in the coconut cream. Season to taste with salt and sugar. Cook, uncovered, for 5–10 mins to reduce the liquid.

5 Serve with steamed rice or roti.

Tip: The curry tastes even better if left overnight for the flavours to develop.

*See 'Basics' on page 167 for how to prepare toasted belachan. Alternatively, some Asian supermarkets stock pre-toasted belachan (e.g. Jeeny's brand).

Facing page features a pottery dish, hand-made by Jeanie (1980s)

There are many different variations of beef rendang curry. My version has been tweaked over the years from Indonesian and Malaysian influences. It is a favourite in my household so I often make a large batch and freeze small portions as backups.

Beef Rendang

SERVES 4

Spice Paste

10–15 dried red chillies, deseeded, soaked

½ tsp –1 tsp black peppercorns, crushed

10 g (⅜ oz) fresh ginger (approx. 2.5 cm (1") piece)

5 g (⅛ oz) fresh turmeric (approx. 2.5 cm (1") piece)

5 cloves garlic

5 shallots (eschalots), or 150–200 g (5¼–7 oz) small pickling onions, or 1 large brown onion

15 g (½ oz) fresh galangal (approx. 4 cm (1½") piece)

4 stalks lemongrass, white part only, chopped

4 pieces candlenuts or macadamias, smashed

3 tsp coriander powder / ground coriander

1 tsp fennel seed powder / ground fennel seeds

1 tsp chilli powder (optional)

4 Tbsp (80 mL) oil

1 cinnamon quill (optional)

1 kg (2 lb 3 oz) beef chuck steak, cut into 2.5 cm x 5 cm (1" x 2") pieces

1 x 400 mL (13½ fl oz) can coconut milk (remove top cream, set aside)

2 tsp tamarind puree

1–1½ cups water

3 Tbsp desiccated coconut

2 tsp salt, or to taste

1 Tbsp sugar, or to taste

1 Place the chillies, peppercorns, ginger, turmeric, garlic, shallots, galangal, lemongrass and candlenuts in a food processor. Process to a fine paste. Add the coriander, fennel and chilli powders.

2 Heat the oil in a large pot and fry the spice paste and cinnamon quill on low heat until fragrant.

3 Add the meat in, increase the heat and fry for 5–10 mins until lightly browned.

4 Add the coconut milk, tamarind puree and water. Simmer, uncovered, on medium heat, until the meat is almost cooked (1–1½ hours). Stir occasionally.

5 Meanwhile, put 3 Tbsp desiccated coconut in a small frypan and toast it over low heat until lightly browned (kerisik). Pulse the kerisik in a spice grinder to fine crumbs. Set aside.

6 Add the reserved coconut cream and kerisik to the meat and continue to cook, uncovered, until the meat is tender. Add in the salt and sugar. Increase the heat and cook until the sauce is reduced and creamy, but not dry.

7 Taste and adjust seasoning before serving. Serve with steamed rice.

Notes:

Cook this curry in advance to allow the flavours to develop. This dish keeps well in the fridge or freezer.

'Kerisik' refers to toasted desiccated coconut. It acts as a thickener and enhances the flavour of the curry.

Thai Green Curry Chicken

This recipe calls for a fresh green curry paste for a fragrant, bright and bold curry. Once you've made the curry paste, composing the rest of the curry is relatively simple; and the resulting taste is authentic and full-flavoured. If you have the time to make your own homemade, from-scratch, curry paste, please give it a try (see Green Curry Paste recipe on page 166). The flavour and fragrance from the fresh ingredients are certainly worth the effort.

SERVES 4

- 300 g (10½ oz) chicken breast or thigh fillets
- 250 mL (8½ fl oz) thick coconut milk / coconut cream (reserve 2 Tbsp for garnish)
- 250 mL (8½ fl oz) thin coconut milk
- 100 g (3½ oz) fresh green curry paste (see Green Curry Paste recipe on page 166)
- 1 eggplant (aubergine), cut into 1.3 cm (½") pieces
- 50 g (1¾ oz) small Thai eggplants, quartered
- 40 g (1⅜ oz) shaved palm sugar, or to taste
- 2 Tbsp fish sauce
- 3 kaffir lime leaves, stem removed, torn into pieces
- 1 cup Thai basil leaves*
- 1 fresh red chilli, sliced lengthwise

1 Slice the chicken thinly and set aside. Put the thick coconut milk in a saucepan and fry over low heat until the oil separates.

2 Then add the green curry paste and fry for 1–2 mins until aromatic.

3 Add the chicken in and cook until it changes colour (turns white). Then add the thin coconut milk, and when it is boiling, add in the big and small eggplants. Simmer for 5–6 mins until the eggplants are slightly soft.

4 Add the palm sugar along the side of the pot so that it melts. Add the fish sauce, lime leaves and half of the Thai basil leaves. Mix in well.

5 Turn off the heat. Dish up and garnish with the remaining Thai basil, red chillies and the reserved coconut cream.

6 Serve with steamed rice.

Note: If you don't have time to make your own curry paste, you can substitute with a good quality store-bought one, e.g. Maesri brand.

Tip: Good quality brands of canned coconut milk and coconut cream include Ayam and Kara. You will notice the difference in fragrance and purity.

*Thai basil has more of an aniseed flavour than regular basil.

Tung Kwa Tong ~ Winter Melon Soup

A cooling (yin) and nutritious soup. Normally served on special occasions. You can find winter melons in Asian grocery stores and selected fruit and vegetable shops.

SERVES 8

2 chicken carcasses (chicken frames)

1 kg (2 lb 3 oz) pork meaty bones

3 slices ginger

2 litres (8 cups) water

12 dried red dates (hung zou), pitted

700 g (1 lb 9 oz) winter melon (tung kwa)

6 dried shiitake mushrooms, rinsed and soaked in water till soft

3 dried scallops, rinsed and soaked in water

12 fresh prawns (shelled), or frozen prawns (defrosted)

200 g (7 oz) cooked ham

2 Tbsp dried goji berries (wolfberries), rinsed

Salt, to taste

1 green shallot (green onion / scallion), chopped, to garnish (optional)

1   Bring a large pot of water to the boil. Blanch the chicken carcasses and pork meaty bones for 15 mins to remove any impurities and scum. Pour away the water and clean the bones in cold water.

2   Put the bones in a large stock pot with 2 litres (8 cups) of water and bring it to the boil. Add in the ginger and red dates and vigorous simmer / gentle boil for 1 hour.

3   Meanwhile, remove the skin of the melon and cut into 2 cm (¾") chunks or cubes. Dice the rehydrated mushrooms, flake the scallops (reserve the water for stock), cut the prawns into 1 cm (⅜") pieces, and dice the ham into 1 cm (⅜") cubes.

4   Strain the soup base into a clean pot, discard the bones. Heat up the soup, put in the melon, mushrooms, scallops, scallop water, ham and goji berries and simmer for 15 mins. Then add the chopped prawns. Season to taste.

5   Serve hot, sprinkled with some green shallots for garnish.

Facing page features a traditional Chinese soup tureen and soup ladle (1970s). A wedding gift from Eddie's mother.

1. Yee mei (Chinese pearl barley) 2. Bing tong (rock sugar) 3. Bak hup (lily bulbs) 4. Mut zou (honey date) 5. Lin yoke (dried longan) 6. Wai san (Chinese yam) 7. Lin chi (lotus seed) 8. Yoke jook (Solomon's seal rhizome) 9. Goji berries 10. See sut (fox nut)

Ching Bo Leung
~ Nourishing Herbal Soup

This nourishing soup is believed by the Chinese to detoxify the body, nourish the kidneys and lungs, and build up the blood. It can be enjoyed hot as a soup, or cold as a sweetened drink, omitting the meat.

SERVES 6

20 g (¾ oz) bak hup (lily bulbs)
25 g (⅞ oz) yee mei (Chinese pearl barley)
38 g (1¼ oz) wai san (Chinese yam)
15 g (½ oz) yoke jook (Solomon's seal rhizome)
10 g (⅜ oz) lin chi (lotus seed)
15 g (½ oz) see sut (fox nut)
15 g (½ oz) lin yoke (dried longan)
2 pieces mut zou (honey date)
500 g (1 lb 2 oz) lean pork shin, or pork bones (if making as a soup)
2 litres (8 cups) water
15g (½ oz) goji berries (wolfberries)

1. Wash and drain the herbs (the first 8 ingredients). Wash the pork.

2. Put the ingredients into a stock pot with 2 litres of water. Bring to the boil on high heat. Skim off any scum that rises to the surface. Reduce heat to a gentle boil for 1½–2 hours.

3. Rinse the goji berries and add them in the last 15 minutes of cooking time.

4. Serve the soup hot.

Tips:
If using pork bones to make the soup, get some with meat on it — it's more flavoursome.
Individual herbs are available from Asian grocery stores.
You can also purchase pre-portioned "Herbal Soup Mix (Ching Bo Leung)" packs from Asian grocery stores.

Variation:
'Ching bo leung' could also be consumed as a cooling drink for the body.

 Gentle-boil the herbs without the meat for 1 hour with 2 litres of water. Add rock sugar (bing tong) to sweeten. Serve warm or cold.

Desserts *and* Cakes

Daan Taat ~ Egg Tarts (v)

These Chinese egg tarts are a real favourite in many families. The tart pastry recipe shared here is easier to make than the more tedious flaky pastry found in yum cha or dim sum restaurants.

MAKES 11 TARTS

90 g (3⅛ oz) sugar
150 mL (5 fl oz) hot water
3 large eggs (min. 50 g (1¾ oz) each)
100 mL (3⅜ fl oz) evaporated milk (e.g. Carnation brand)
½ tsp vanilla extract

180 g (6⅜ oz) cake flour, or plain flour (all-purpose flour)
25 g (⅞ oz) caster sugar (superfine sugar)
100 g (3½ oz) unsalted butter, softened
⅛ tsp salt
2 Tbsp beaten egg (reserved)

11 individual, fluted, egg tart tins

Custard

1 Put the sugar and hot water in a small saucepan. Stir to dissolve the sugar.

2 Beat the 3 eggs in a medium mixing bowl. Reserve 2 Tbsp of the beaten egg for making the tart pastry. Set aside.

3 Add the sugar syrup, evaporated milk and vanilla to the eggs. Mix with a whisk until smooth. Strain the mixture twice through a fine sieve. Chill in the fridge.

Tart Cases

4 Sift together the flour and sugar in a large mixing bowl. Add the softened butter and beat with a wooden spoon until the butter is incorporated into the flour. Add the reserved 2 Tbsp egg and mix in. Knead by hand for 2–3 mins until the dough is smooth. Shape into an oval disc. Cling wrap it and chill in the fridge for at least 30 mins.

5 Preheat oven to 180°C (360°F).

6 Take the dough out of the fridge. Roll the dough into a log and cut it into 11 pieces (about 30–31 g (1 oz) each). Roll each piece into a ball.

7 Place a pastry ball in the middle of the tart tin. Using your thumb, press the dough out gently and evenly to cover the base and sides of the tart tin. Repeat with the rest of the pastry balls and tart tins.

8 Transfer the custard filling (egg mixture) to a jug for easy pouring. Fill each tart case to about 95% full. Place them on a baking tray.

9 Bake in preheated oven for 25–30 mins or until set. Remove from oven and allow to cool slightly before turning each tart out from their tin. Can be eaten warm or cold.

Tips:

Custard will continue cooking after you remove it from the oven, so watch that it doesn't overbake.

The specialised egg tart tins can be found in Asian supermarkets or kitchenware stores. Traditionally, they have fluted sides, distinct ridges, a fixed base and are made of aluminium.

Facing page features a pottery sashimi plate, hand-made by Jeanie (1980s)

One of my daughter's earliest childhood memories is of me making batches and batches of these egg tarts with our neighbour in Canberra, until every kitchen surface was covered.

Kow Chan Goh ~ Nine Layer Kuih (V)

'Kuih' (pronounced "kway") broadly means 'cake' and encompasses a wide variety of bite-sized snacks or desserts. In this case, it's a Malaysian steamed layer cake, made with rice flour, coconut milk and a sugar syrup infused with pandan.

As a child, it was always fun to peel the individual layers apart and eat them one by one. In the past, 'kuih' were mainly made for festive celebrations. But nowadays, 'kuih' are available at any time of day as desserts and snacks in tea rooms and cake shops, along with other varieties of sweets.

SERVES 6–8

180 g (6⅜ oz) rice flour (not glutinous)
150 mL (5 fl oz) water

Syrup
190 g (6¾ oz) sugar
400 mL (13½ fl oz) water
3 pandan leaves (screwpine leaves), knotted

200 mL (6¾ fl oz) santan* (e.g. Kara brand)
⅛ tsp salt
Pink food colouring
Orange-red food colouring

*'Santan' refers to coconut cream or thick coconut milk.

1 Combine the rice flour and water in a mixing bowl. Stir and leave to soak for an hour.

2 Make the syrup. Boil together the sugar, water and pandan leaves. When all the sugar has dissolved, remove from heat and cool.

3 Add the sugar syrup, santan and salt to the soaked rice flour in the mixing bowl. Stir and mix well. Strain and divide the mixture into two bowls. Colour one portion pink.

4 Grease a 20 cm (8") round pan. Put it in a steamer to heat up for 5 mins.

5 Pour half a cup of the white batter in the heated pan. Steam, covered, for 4½–5 mins or until set. Then pour half a cup of the pink batter over the white layer and steam, covered, for 4½ mins or until set. Repeat, alternating the white and pink layers.

Note: 4–5 mins is sufficient to set each layer. If steamed too long, the layers may fail to bind to each other.

6 Colour the last (9th) layer orange-red. Pour it over the previous layer and steam, covered, for 4½ mins.

7 After the last layer is set, steam the whole cake for a further 15 mins, opening the lid every 5 mins.

Note: This is to let the steam out so as not to overcook the cake.
Tip: Top up the water level in the steamer. Do not let it boil dry.

8 Test by lightly touching the top of the cake with your fingers. The kuih (cake) is done if it doesn't stick to your fingers.

9 Remove from heat and cool completely before cutting into diamond shapes using a serrated cutter.

Facing page features matching Chinese teacups from Eddie's teapot set (1968)

Chinese Almond Cookies (v)

These nutty little cookies are crisp when you first bite them, then give way to a crumbly, melt-in-the-mouth texture. Almond cookies are great to serve at Chinese New Year when family and friends come to visit, or to package up and give as gifts.

MAKES APPROX. 50 COOKIES

3 cups (450 g) plain flour (all-purpose flour)

1½ cups (240 g) pure icing sugar (powdered sugar)

100 g (3½ oz) almond meal / ground almonds

100 g (3½ oz) crushed almonds

1 cup + 1 Tbsp (270 mL) neutral oil (e.g. vegetable, canola, rice bran)

1 egg, lightly beaten, for glaze

1 Preheat oven to 180°C (360°F) and line 2 baking trays (cookie sheets) with baking paper.

2 Mix the dry ingredients together in a mixing bowl. Add the oil and stir with a spoon until the dry ingredients are incorporated in the oil.

3 Put 2 teaspoons of mixture into your palm. Cup your palm and press the dough together with your fingers. Form into a round by pressing, kneading and shaping into a slightly domed 3 cm (1⅛") disc. Place onto a lined baking tray. Repeat with the remaining mixture to form about 50 cookies.

4 Press the top of each cookie lightly with your finger to indent it. Brush the tops with the beaten egg.

5 Bake in preheated oven for 20 mins. Remove from oven and transfer to racks to cool.

6 Cool the cookies completely before putting in containers.

Sago Snowballs *or* Sago Slices (V)

A dessert, or snack, that can be made ahead and kept in the fridge. They're great for parties, too.

MAKES 20–25 PIECES

1 packet (375 g, 13¼ oz) sago / tapioca pearls (e.g. Cock brand)
2 cups (500 mL) water
1 can (400 mL, 13½ fl oz) coconut milk
1½ cans (600 mL) fresh milk, or 600 mL (20 fl oz) evaporated milk (e.g. Carnation brand)
1½ cups (330 g) caster sugar (superfine sugar)
1 packet (500 g, 1 lb 2 oz) desiccated coconut

1 Combine the sago with 2 cups of water and 1 can of coconut milk in a large pot. Leave to soak for 2 hours.

2 Add in 1½ cans of fresh milk (using the empty can to measure) or evaporated milk. Stir well.

3 Cook over medium–high heat until the sago is transparent, stirring continuously or it will burn at the bottom. Cook for about 10–15 mins. Mixture will be thick at this stage.

4 Add in the sugar, stir and continue to cook until the sugar is completely dissolved. Remove from heat.

5 Put 1 Tbsp sago mixture into each mini muffin pan. Let them cool slightly, then remove and roll into a ball and coat with desiccated coconut. Place the snowballs into patty cases. Refrigerate until ready to serve.

Sago Slices

Follow above steps 1 to 4.

5 Pour the sago mixture into a lamington tray (20 cm x 30 cm / 8" x 12"). Level it out, then coat the top layer with desiccated coconut. Do this quickly as the surface dries fast, forming a skin, and the coconut may not stick well when set.

6 Cool completely. Refrigerate.

7 When set, cut into squares then coat the sides and bottom of each slice with coconut. Refrigerate until ready to serve.

Jeanie's Mango Pudding

Often seen on yum cha or dim sum dessert carts, you can now enjoy Chinese mango pudding at home. A quick and easy dessert to make ahead. Pop it into the fridge until ready to serve. It's a great one to make during mango season.

SERVES 8

250 g (8¾ oz) mango, pureed

150 mL (5 fl oz) evaporated milk (e.g. Carnation brand)

125 mL (4¼ fl oz) fresh cream (pouring cream)

300 mL (10 fl oz) ice cubes

200 g (7 oz) mango, cut into small cubes

2 Tbsp (26 g) powdered gelatine

⅔ cup (145 g) sugar

300 mL (10 fl oz) hot water

1 Mix together the mango puree, evaporated milk, cream, ice cubes and mango cubes in a large mixing bowl.

2 Stir the gelatine and sugar in the hot water until dissolved.

3 Pour the hot gelatine mixture into the mango mixture and stir until the ice cubes melt and the pudding mixture is starting to set.

4 Pour the pudding mixture into a jelly mould, or individual cups / moulds. Refrigerate until set.

5 Turn out the pudding, cut into slices and serve with a dollop of cream or ice cream, if desired. Or serve in individual cups.

Tip: Use overripe, soft mangoes for the puree and firmer, ripe mangoes for the cubes.

Note: For a firmer jelly, add an extra teaspoon of gelatine.

Facing page features plates from Jeanie's china tea sets (1970s)

Almond Jelly *with* Longan

When my children were young, I often made this dessert for them. As a variation, I would sometimes omit the almond essence and call it 'milk jelly'. Traditionally, almond jelly is made with agar agar, but this was hard to find in Australia in the 1970s so I adapted the recipe to use gelatine.

SERVES 6

2 Tbsp (26 g) powdered gelatine
120 mL (4 fl oz) hot water
3 cups (750 mL) milk or almond milk
3½ Tbsp sugar
1 tsp almond essence
1 tin longan or lychee, to serve (e.g. Aroy-D brand)

1 Dissolve the gelatine in the hot water.

2 Warm the milk on the stove, add the sugar and essence. Stir in the gelatine mixture.

3 Pour into a 20 cm x 25 cm (8" x 10") rectangular tray or into individual moulds.

4 Chill until set. Cut into diamond shapes or cubes.

5 Serve with longan, lychee, or fruits of choice.

For vegetarians – replace the gelatine in this recipe with agar agar.

For vegans or those with lactose intolerance – this recipe can be successfully created with almond milk.

Bubur Cha-Cha ~ Sweet Potato *and* Taro in Coconut Milk ⓥ

Pronounced "bo bo cha cha", this dessert soup is a lesser-known dessert outside of southeast Asia, but a real favourite among Malaysians and Singaporeans.

SERVES 6–8

- 50 g (1¾ oz) dried black-eyed beans
- 8 pandan leaves (screwpine leaves), knotted
- 9 cups (2.25 litres) water
- 400 mL (13½ fl oz) coconut milk
- 350 g (12¼ oz) sweet potato (kumara), cut into 1½ cm (⅝") pieces
- 350 g (12¼ oz) taro, cut into 1½ cm (⅝") pieces
- 150 g (5¼ oz) white sugar (granulated sugar)
- 2 Tbsp sago / tapioca pearls, rinsed of starch

1 Wash the black-eyed beans and soak 1 hour prior.

2 Put the pandan leaves and water in a large saucepan. Bring to a boil. Drain the beans and put them in to cook till soft. Lower the heat, add in the coconut milk. Stir. Keep warm.

3 Steam the sweet potato and taro separately. They should be just tender (not soft) as they will be cooked in the syrup later on.

4 Bring the pandan coconut water to the boil. Add the sugar in and stir to dissolve. Put in the sago, sweet potato and taro. Stir gently. Lower heat and let it simmer for 10 mins.

5 Remove the pandan leaves. Test for sweetness. Serve warm.

Sago with Gula Melaka ⓥ

A cooling dessert after a spicy meal. This dessert is also popular with kids who will enjoy the sweetened coconut flavour and the texture of the sago pearls.

SERVES 4

120 g (4¼ oz) sago / tapioca pearls (e.g. Cock brand)

1 small can santan / coconut cream (e.g. Kara brand)

A pinch of salt

Syrup

600 mL (20 fl oz) water

5 Tbsp shaved gula melaka* (Malaysian palm sugar)

3 Tbsp sugar

2 pandan leaves (screwpine leaves), knotted, or pandan essence

*If you can't find gula melaka, then you could replace with brown sugar, but the flavour will be a little different.

1 Wash the sago and soak for 5 mins. When the sago is soft and swollen, drain well.

2 Boil 2 litres (8 cups) of water in a saucepan.

3 Put the sago in the boiling water. Cook till sago is soft and transparent, about 20–25 mins. Remove from heat. Tip into a strainer to drain off the water. Rinse under cold tap water to wash off the excess starch. Do it in 2 or 3 lots if you do not have a big strainer. Put the sago in a large container.

4 Spoon the sago into small moulds. Press gently to compact. Chill in the fridge.

5 Put the syrup ingredients into a saucepan. Cook the syrup until the gula melaka and sugar have dissolved. Chill the syrup.

6 Add a pinch of salt to the santan.

7 To serve, turn out the sago from their moulds into ice-cream glasses or dessert bowls. Pour in 3 Tbsp syrup followed by 2 Tbsp of santan for each bowl. To eat, mix the sago into the syrup and coconut milk.

8 Serve cold after a hot curry meal.

Notes:

'Santan' refers to coconut cream / thick coconut milk.

'Gula melaka' refers to Malaysian coconut palm sugar. It can be found in Asian grocery stores or Asian supermarkets. A close relative is the Indonesian palm sugar 'gula jawa'. The Thai palm sugar 'nam tan puek' is lighter in colour and flavour than gula melaka.

Facing page features Jeanie's Crown Corning sweet or seafood bowls (1980s)

Green Papaya *and* Longan Dessert Soup Ⓥ

Green papaya has been used for generations for many therapeutic effects. Other ingredients can be substituted or added such as snow fungus or goji berries (wolfberries).

SERVES 6

300 g (10½ oz) green papaya

12 pieces dried red dates (hung zou), pitted

18 pieces dried longan (lin yoke)

1.5 litres (6 cups) water

Rock sugar, or raw sugar, to taste

1 Peel the papaya, remove the seeds and white core. Cut the papaya into 1.5 cm (⅝") chunks.

2 Rinse the red dates and the longans. Put them in a large pot with 1.5 litres of water. Bring to the boil.

3 Add in the papaya and cook until the papaya is tender.

4 Add rock sugar or raw sugar to sweeten, if desired. Serve hot or cold.

....

Variations:

If using dried snow fungus (syut yee), also called silver ear fungus, soak it until soft, cut off the hard ends and cut into smaller pieces. Add them in at step 2.

If using dried goji berries (wolfberries), rinse them, then add them in 10–15 minutes before serving.

Hung Dau Saa
~ Sweet Red Bean Soup ⓥ

Served warm at the end of the meal as a dessert soup (tong soei).

SERVES 4–6

200 g (7 oz) red adzuki beans

100 g (3½ oz) green mung beans (optional)

2 litres (8 cups) water

3 pandan leaves (screwpine leaves), knotted, or 2 pieces mandarin peel (optional)

Brown slab sugar, or white sugar (granulated sugar), to taste

1 Wash the red and green beans. Soak the beans for 1 hour.

2 Bring the water and pandan leaves (or mandarin peel) to the boil in a pot.

3 Add in the beans. Cook at a gentle boil for about an hour, until the beans are soft and tender. If the beans are still hard, add more water and continue cooking until soft.

4 Add in the sugar, to taste.

5 Serve warm or cold.

....

Variations:

This recipe can easily be varied to suit your preferences. You can omit the mung beans and use only adzuki beans (300 g); or substitute the mung beans with black-eyed beans; or add lily bulbs, lotus seeds, or dried longans, if you like.

Mango *with* Sticky Rice ⓥ

A lovely dessert to finish off with after a hot Thai meal.

SERVES 3–4

1 cup glutinous rice
125 mL (½ cup) thick coconut milk
50 g (¼ cup) sugar
⅛ tsp salt
1 mango
1 tsp sesame seeds, toasted* (optional)

60 mL (¼ cup) thin coconut milk
3 tsp sugar
Pinch of salt

1 Soak the glutinous rice (sticky rice) in water overnight.

2 The next day, drain and rinse the rice. Then steam the glutinous rice for 20–30 mins until cooked.

3 Mix the thick coconut milk, sugar and salt together in a bowl.

4 Once the rice is cooked, transfer it to a bowl or container. Add the coconut milk, sugar and salt mixture while the rice is still hot and combine thoroughly. Rest for about 30–40 mins to allow the rice to absorb the coconut milk.

Sauce

5 Mix the sauce ingredients together. Set aside.

6 Peel the mango, cut the cheeks from the seed and slice the mango cheeks thinly. Allow 6 slices of mango per portion.

7 To serve, divide the sticky rice into 4 portions. Place the mango slices on top of or beside the rice. Pour the thin coconut sauce over the mangoes and sprinkle sesame seeds on top, if desired.

Note: Start this recipe the night before.

*To toast sesame seeds: dry fry the seeds in a frypan over low heat until lightly toasted.

Crème Caramel ⓥ

A classic dessert no one can resist! Adapted from a 1986 Family Circle magazine clipping, this trusted recipe has been prepared for countless dinner parties and family gatherings over the years.

SERVES 6–8

¾ cup (165 g) sugar
¾ cup (188 mL) water

6 extra large eggs (min. 59 g (2 oz) each)
2 tsp vanilla extract
⅓ cup (75 g) caster sugar (superfine sugar)
425 mL (14½ fl oz) milk
300 mL (10 fl oz) fresh cream (pouring cream)

Caramel

1 Combine the sugar and water in a small saucepan. Stir over low heat until the sugar is dissolved. Bring to the boil. Boil rapidly without stirring until the sugar mixture turns golden brown. Do not stir. Turn off the heat and pour the caramel into a deep 20 cm (8") round cake tin, quickly rotating the tin so that the caramel coats the base of the tin. The caramel will set after a few minutes.

Tip: Wear oven mitts when rotating the caramel as the cake tin gets hot.

2 Preheat oven to 150°C (300°F).

Custard

3 Lightly whisk the eggs, vanilla and sugar in a mixing bowl.

4 Combine the milk and cream in a medium saucepan over medium heat. Bring to scalding point. When bubbles start to appear around the edge of the pan, remove from heat. Cool slightly.

5 Add the milk and cream mixture to the egg mixture while mixing with a whisk.

6 Pour the custard mixture through a sieve over the caramel in the tin.

7 Place the tin in a baking dish with boiling water to come halfway up the sides of the tin (making a bain-marie / water bath). Bake in preheated oven for 40 mins or until just set. The custard will firm up on cooling.

8 Remove from bain-marie and stand for several hours to cool before refrigerating.

9 To serve, run a thin bladed knife around the edge of the tin. Position a rimmed plate or platter over the top of the cake tin. Flip both over and turn the custard out onto the serving platter, allowing the caramel to run down the sides. Slice into wedges and serve with some caramel spooned over.

Facing page features Nanna Brab's silver spoon

Pavlova ⓥ

Pavlova is a long-time favourite of our family and I have been making it this way for years. Perfect for any celebration such as Christmas or birthdays.

SERVES 8

4 egg whites
1 cup (220 g) caster sugar (superfine sugar)
1 Tbsp cornflour (cornstarch)
1 tsp white vinegar

Topping
300 mL (10 fl oz) thickened cream
¼ cup (40 g) icing sugar (powdered sugar)
1 tsp vanilla
Fruits of choice

Tips:
Don't use freshly laid eggs, week-old eggs whip up better.

Separate eggs straight from the fridge, then bring to room temperature.

This recipe produces a more delicate, crispy shell, but is more likely to crack. If you want a thicker, stronger shell, reduce the oven temperature to 120°C (250°F) and bake for 1–1¼ hours.

1 Preheat oven to 150°C (300°F). Using a round pan base as a guide, trace a 23 cm (9") diameter circle on baking paper. Turn the paper over and place on a baking tray (cookie sheet).

2 Whip up the egg whites until soft peaks form. Add the caster sugar in gradually, beating constantly after each addition. Beat until the sugar has dissolved. Fold in the cornflour and vinegar.

3 Dab some meringue on the corners of the baking tray to hold the baking paper down. Spread the meringue mixture onto the circle on the baking paper. Shape the meringue evenly into a dome-like shape with a palette knife. Run the palette knife up the outer edge of the meringue making curved furrows for a decorative finish.

4 Bake in preheated oven for 40 mins or until crisp. Turn off oven, cool pavlova in oven with door slightly ajar.

5 For the topping, put the cream in a medium bowl. Add the icing sugar and vanilla. Beat until thick and smooth.

6 Spread the whipped cream on top of the pavlova. Decorate with fruits of choice, e.g. strawberries, blueberries, raspberries, kiwifruit, passionfruit, etc.

Facing page features Jeanie's retro tea towel

Jeanie's Chiffon Cake ⓥ

A light and moist sponge, this is a tried-and-true recipe that has been made countless times for the enjoyment of many friends and family. My most often requested recipe, I have tweaked it over time to be the best it can be.

SERVES 12

1 cup (150 g, 5¼ oz) self-raising flour
1 Tbsp cornflour (cornstarch)
½ tsp baking powder
7 extra large eggs (min. 59 g (2 oz) each)
½ tsp cream of tartar
¾ cup + 1 Tbsp (180 g, 6⅜ oz) caster sugar (superfine sugar)
125 mL (½ cup, 4¼ fl oz) neutral oil (e.g. rice bran, canola)
2 tsp vanilla essence
125 mL (½ cup, 4¼ fl oz) milk or water

Aluminum chiffon / angel cake tin 23–25 cm (9–10")

Tip: It's important not to grease your chiffon tin, otherwise the cake will slip out and collapse when inverted.

1 Preheat oven to 200°C (400°F). Have a chiffon cake tin ready, ungreased.

2 Sift the self-raising flour, cornflour and baking powder three times. Set aside.

3 Separate the eggs.

4 In the first mixing bowl: beat the egg whites and cream of tartar until foamy. Gradually add half the sugar and beat until stiff and smooth, like meringue.

5 In the second mixing bowl: beat together the egg yolks and remaining sugar until light. Then add in the oil, vanilla, milk or water and sifted flours and beat on low speed until smooth — about 2 mins. Mixture should be thick, smooth and runny.

6 Add one third of the meringue to the egg and flour mixture. Fold in gently on low speed. Remove the beaters. Add another third of the meringue and fold in lightly with a metal spoon. Repeat with the remaining meringue. Make sure the meringue is well incorporated into the batter.

7 Pour the cake batter into the chiffon tin. Bang a couple of times on the table to let out any big air bubbles.

8 Put into preheated oven. Reduce heat to 180°C (360°F) and bake for 10 mins. Reduce heat to 160°C (320°F) and bake for a further 35 mins, or until a skewer inserted in the cake comes out clean.

9 When cooked, remove from oven and invert the chiffon tin on your benchtop, leaving it upside down for an hour to cool. This allows the cake to hang in the tin, so it does not deflate.

10 To remove the cake, run a thin-bladed knife along the centre funnel and outer edge of the cake tin. Holding the centre funnel, lift the cake from the outer tin. Run the knife along the base of the tin. Invert the cake on your palm, remove the tin base, and place the cake top-down onto a serving plate.

Facing page features Nanna Brab's Royal Albert fine china plates

Apple Tea Cake

Adapted from an Australian Women's Weekly recipe for apple cake, this is a simple but sturdy tea cake, perfect for morning tea or an afternoon snack.

SERVES 8

185 g (6½ oz) unsalted butter, softened

165 g (¾ cup) caster sugar (superfine sugar)

2 tsp lemon rind, grated

3 extra large eggs (min. 59 g (2 oz) each)

150 g (1 cup) self-raising flour, sifted

65 g (½ cup) spelt flour, sifted

80 mL (⅓ cup) milk

2 small green apples (e.g. Granny Smith)

1 tsp powdered gelatine

2 Tbsp hot water

2 Tbsp apricot jam, strained

1 Preheat oven to 180°C (360°F) and line a 20 cm (8") round cake pan.

2 Cream the butter, sugar and rind in a small bowl until light and fluffy. Beat in the eggs, one at a time, until combined. Transfer the mixture to a large bowl.

3 Fold in the sifted flours and milk. Spread the mixture into the prepared cake pan.

4 Peel the apples, cut into quarters and remove cores. Cut slits into the rounded sides of the apple quarters — about three-quarters of the way through.

5 Arrange the apple quarters, rounded side up, around the edge of the cake. Bake in preheated oven for about 1 hour, or until a skewer inserted in the middle comes out clean. Remove from oven.

6 Sprinkle the gelatine over the hot water to dissolve. Add the jam and mix. Spread half the jam mixture over the hot cake. Cool the cake in the pan.

7 Remove the cooled cake from the pan and brush the remaining warmed jam mixture over the top.

Facing page features Nanna Brab's Royal Albert fine china tea set

Hazelnut Apple Cake *with* Lemon Icing ⓥ

SERVES 8

185 g (6½ oz) unsalted butter, softened

⅔ cup (150 g) caster sugar (superfine sugar)

3 large eggs (min. 50 g (1¾ oz) each)

2 Tbsp Dutch cocoa, sifted

½ cup (75 g) self-raising flour

185 g (6½ oz) hazelnut meal / ground hazelnuts

1 apple, grated (e.g. Granny Smith, Gala)

60 g (2 oz) unsalted butter, softened

1 cup (160 g) icing sugar (powdered sugar), sifted

1 Tbsp lemon juice

1 Preheat oven to 170°C (340°F). Line or grease a deep 20 cm (8") round cake pan.

2 Cream the butter and sugar in a small bowl until light and fluffy.

3 Beat in the eggs, one at a time, until combined. Transfer the mixture to a large mixing bowl. Fold in the sifted cocoa, self-raising flour, hazelnut meal and grated apple.

4 Spread the cake mixture into the prepared pan. Bake in preheated oven for about 55 mins, or until a skewer inserted in the middle comes out clean. Remove the cake from the oven and rest for 5 mins. Turn the cake out onto a wire rack to cool completely.

Lemon Icing

5 Beat the butter in a small bowl until light and fluffy. Beat in the sifted icing sugar, then enough lemon juice to give a spreadable consistency.

6 Spread the cooled cake with the lemon icing.

Facing page features Jeanie's Noritake china teacups and saucers from Japan

Pineapple *and* Apple Slice ⓥ

An old favourite, adapted from a 1982 magazine clipping featuring Ethel Brice's Cookery School, this delicious recipe is easy to make and brings back memories of after-school treats. This recipe was one of the first that I allowed my kids to make in the kitchen when learning how to cook.

MAKES 24 SLICES

- 185 g (6½ oz) unsalted butter, softened
- 165 g (¾ cup) caster sugar (superfine sugar)
- 2 tsp lemon rind, grated
- 2 extra large eggs (min. 59 g (2 oz) each)
- 1 tsp vanilla extract
- 225 g (1½ cups) plain flour (all-purpose flour)
- 1 x 470 g (1 lb) can crushed pineapple, drained thoroughly
- 3 cooking apples, peeled, sliced and lightly cooked, or 1 x 470 g (1 lb) can pie apples, drained

1. Preheat oven to 180°C (360°F) and grease a lamington tin (20 cm x 30 cm / 8" x 12") or slab tin (20 cm x 25 cm / 8" x 10").

2. Beat the butter, sugar and lemon rind until creamy.

3. Add the eggs, one at a time, beating well after each addition. Add in the vanilla and the flour and mix in.

4. Spread half the cake mixture into the prepared tin.

5. Mix the drained pineapple and apples together in a bowl. Spoon over the cake mixture in the tin, spreading the fruit out evenly.

6. Add the rest of the cake mixture on top of the fruits. It's not necessary to spread evenly, it will spread over the fruits as it cooks.

7. Bake in preheated oven for 45–50 mins or until browned.

8. Remove and cool in tin. Cut into squares, dust with icing sugar and serve warm or cold with a dollop of cream or ice cream as a dessert, or as an afternoon treat with a cup of tea.

Facing page features china teacups and saucers from Maud ("Ffrosty"), and pieces from Royal Albert china tea set from Nanna Brab

Seeded Oaty Slice ⓥ

Adapted from an old Australian Women's Weekly recipe, this slice is wholesome and not-too-sweet. It keeps well and is great to pull out for the munchies, morning tea or to pack in a lunchbox.

MAKES 24 SLICES

1 cup (100 g) rolled oats (old-fashioned oats)

1 cup (150 g) plain flour (all-purpose flour)

¾ cup (60 g) desiccated coconut

½ cup (110 g) raw sugar

1 cup mixed seeds (e.g. pepita, sunflower, linseed, chia), or mixed nuts (e.g. almonds, walnuts, pecans, etc.)

½ cup vegetable oil, or 125 g (4½ oz) unsalted butter

3 Tbsp honey

3 Tbsp water

½ tsp bicarbonate of soda

1 Preheat oven to 180°C (360°F). Grease or line a 25 cm x 30 cm (10" x 12") Swiss roll pan.

2 Combine the oats, flour, coconut, sugar and seeds (or nuts) in a large mixing bowl. If using nuts instead of seeds, roughly chop them.

3 Place the oil (or butter), honey and water in a saucepan. Stir over low heat to combine (or until butter is melted). Stir in the bicarb soda. Pour into the dry ingredients. Stir well to combine.

4 Press the mixture evenly into the prepared pan. Bake in preheated oven for 25 mins. Cool in pan before cutting into slices.

Basics

5-Spice Powder

Make your own 5-spice powder in small batches to keep it fragrant.

1 star anise
1 tsp cloves
1 tsp fennel seeds
1 tsp Sichuan peppercorns (optional)
2 tsp coriander seeds
3 tsp cinnamon powder

Put the spices in a spice grinder and grind to a powder. Store in an airtight container.

Chilli Sauce

300 g (10½ oz) fresh red chillies, deseeded
30 g (3 cloves, 1 oz) garlic
½ tsp salt
4 Tbsp sugar
½ cup (125 mL) vinegar

1 Blend the chillies and garlic to a paste in a small food processor. Remove.

2 Mix all the ingredients in a saucepan and stir over medium heat.

3 Bring to a boil. Cool. Store in sterilised jars. Can keep for up to a year in the fridge.

Fried Shallots (Fried Onions)

20 red shallots (eschalots), finely sliced
Vegetable oil, for deep frying

1 Fill a small saucepan ⅓ full with oil, over medium heat. Drop a piece of sliced shallot in. If it sizzles, it's hot enough.

2 Carefully add all the shallots in. Deep fry, stirring occasionally.

3 Shallots will start to float and turn lightly golden.

4 Turn heat down and watch that the shallots do not burn. As soon as they turn golden brown, remove with a strainer and drain on paper towel. The fried shallots will crisp up on cooling.

Green Curry Paste

In many Asian countries, you can buy freshly-made curry paste of all varieties from the local food market. It's not as readily available here, so we have to make our own. If you have the time to make your own homemade, from-scratch, curry paste, please give it a try. The flavour and fragrance from the fresh ingredients are certainly worth the effort.

Makes 100 g — 130 g (approx. 4 oz) curry paste.

Dry Items

1 tsp coriander seeds
½ tsp cumin seeds
½ tsp black peppercorns
½ tsp salt

Fresh Items

4–5 long green chillies*, deseeded and chopped
2 red shallots (eschalots), chopped
2 stalks lemongrass, white part only, chopped
2 Tbsp fresh galangal, grated with a microplane
5 g (⅛ oz) fresh turmeric, chopped
5 cloves garlic, smashed
2 tsp belachan (dried shrimp paste), toasted^
2 tsp lime zest
2 Tbsp coriander (cilantro) roots and stems#
Extra water or oil, as needed

1 Roast the coriander seeds and cumin seeds in a small frypan over low heat until brown.

2 Put the coriander seeds, cumin seeds and black peppercorns into a spice grinder. Grind to a powder.

3 Blend the fresh and dry items in a blender until smooth. If the curry paste is too dry, add a bit of water or oil.

Tip: It's best to use the curry paste fresh. Or it can be frozen for up to a month.

*Use 20 small Thai green chillies (scuds) for a very spicy curry.

^See facing page for how to prepare toasted belachan. Alternatively, some Asian supermarkets stock pre-toasted belachan (e.g. Jeeny's brand).

#Reserve the coriander leaves as garnish for the cooked curry.

Homemade Chicken Stock

2 chicken carcasses (chicken frames)
2 litres (8 cups) water
1 slice of ginger
1 onion, peeled, left whole

1   Remove any fat from the chicken carcasses and clean them with water.
2   Put all the ingredients into a large stock pot with 2 litres of water.
3   Bring to the boil, reduce heat and simmer for 1–1½ hours.
4   Remove scum and impurities from the surface during cooking.
5   Cool and strain the stock, discard the solids.
6   Refrigerate for up to 5 days or freeze for up to 3 months.

Nam Jim Sauce

2 cloves garlic, peeled
1–2 Thai red chillies, deseeded, chopped
A pinch of salt
2 Tbsp shaved palm sugar
2 Tbsp lime juice
2 Tbsp fish sauce
2–3 kaffir lime leaves, finely sliced

1   Pound the garlic, chillies and salt in a mortar and pestle till fine.
2   Add in the palm sugar, lime juice, fish sauce and lime leaves.
3   Taste and adjust to your liking. It should be hot, sour, salty and sweet. Best to make it fresh and use immediately.

Rempah Paste

200 g (7 oz) red shallots (eschalots)
2 cloves garlic
10 g (⅜ oz) fresh ginger
10 g (⅜ oz) fresh galangal
10 g (⅜ oz) fresh turmeric
2 stalks lemongrass, white part only
10 g (⅜ oz) dried red chillies, deseeded, soaked 30 mins
6–8 fresh red chillies, deseeded
20 g (¾ oz) belachan, toasted
3 candlenuts or macadamias, smashed

1   Chop the above ingredients roughly and put them into a food processor. Process to a fine paste, scraping the sides of the bowl now and then.
2   Use as a base for spicy dishes, e.g. curries, laksa. Store in the refrigerator or freezer.

Roasted Peanuts

1 cup unsalted peanuts

1   Dry fry the nuts in a frypan over low heat, stirring regularly until nuts are lightly browned and cooked through.
2   Cool. Store in an airtight container. Grind or chop as required.

Toasted Belachan

20 g (¾ oz) belachan paste (dried shrimp paste)
Aluminium foil

1   Wrap the belachan in foil tightly. Toast in frypan for 2 mins on each side.
2   It should be dry and crumbly. Use as needed.
3   Wrap any unused portion in foil and keep in the fridge.

Sauces Pantry

To get the right flavour, I've listed some of the items I keep stocked in my sauce cupboard or fridge. Other brands can be substituted, if preferred.

1. Light soy sauce (1st or 2nd extract)
2. Mushroom flavour superior dark soy sauce
3. Usukuchi light colour soy sauce
4. Shaoxing cooking wine
5. Premium fish sauce

⑥ Pure sesame oil	⑪ Premium oyster sauce
⑦ All-purpose soy sauce (for braising)	⑫ Thai sweet chilli sauce
⑧ Hinode mirin	⑬ Hoi sin sauce
⑨ Japanese cooking sake	⑭ Red bean curd (fermented)
⑩ Rice vinegar	⑮ Kecap manis (sweet soy sauce)

⑯ Chinkiang vinegar (for dumplings)
⑰ Coconut cream
⑱ Water chestnut slices
⑲ Organic white miso paste

DRY PANTRY

MAKAN AT MUM'S

170 DRY PANTRY

MAKAN AT MUM'S

Dry Pantry

For an authentic flavour, I've listed here some of the dry goods that I like to keep stocked in my pantry. Other brands can be substituted, if preferred.

1. Rice stick vermicelli noodles (mei fun)
2. Chinese rock sugar
3. Dried shrimps (har mei)
4. Dried cloud ear fungus (wan yee)
5. Thai palm sugar
6. Korean sweet potato starch noodles
7. Chinese brown slab sugar
8. Bean thread vermicelli (fun see)
9. Glutinous rice flour
10. Rice flour (not glutinous)
11. Rice stick noodles (for pad thai, pho, etc.)
12. Belachan (dried shrimp paste)
13. Dried tamarind fruit pieces / tamarind peel
14. Tamarind pulp
15. Dried candlenuts
16. Tapioca pearls / sago
17. Chicken bouillon powder / chicken stock powder
18. Fried shallots (eschalots) / fried onions
19. Wet tamarind pulp / concentrated cooking tamarind

Index

A
Acar Awak 19
Almond Cookies, Chinese 135
Almond Jelly with Longan 140
Apple
    Apple Tea Cake 158
    Hazelnut Apple Cake with Lemon Icing 160
    Pineapple and Apple Slice 163
Apple Tea Cake 158
Assam Laksa 78

B
Bean curd *see* Tofu
Beef
    Beef Broth Noodle Soup (Ching Tong Ngau Larm) 81
    Beef Rendang 121
    Beef Stew with Daikon and Carrots (Mun Ngau Larm) 105
    Braised Beef Shin with Soya Eggs (Hung Siu Ngau Yook) 85
    Thai Beef Salad 35
Beef Broth Noodle Soup 81
Beef Rendang 121
Beijing Spicy Sauce Noodles 69
Belachan, Toasted 167
Belly Pork with Preserved Vegetable 106
Braised Beef Shin with Soya Eggs 85
Braised Belly Pork Ribs with Eggs 103
Braised Tofu with Shiitake Mushrooms 112
Bubur Cha-Cha 142
Buddha's Delight 114

C
Cabbage
    Beijing Spicy Sauce Noodles (Zha Jeung Mein) 69
    Buddha's Delight (New Year Jai) 114
    Malaysian Pickled Vegetables (Acar Awak) 19
    Pan Fried Pork Dumplings (War Tip) 16
    Spring Rolls 12
Cake
    Apple Tea Cake 158
    Egg Tarts (Daan Taat) 130
    Hazelnut Apple Cake with Lemon Icing 160
    Jeanie's Chiffon Cake 157
    Nine Layer Kuih (Kow Chan Goh) 132
    Pavlova 154
    Pineapple and Apple Slice 163
Carrot
    Beef Stew with Daikon and Carrots (Mun Ngau Larm) 105
    Beijing Spicy Sauce Noodles (Zha Jeung Mein) 69
    Korean Sweet Potato Noodles (Jap Chae) 73
    Prosperity Toss Salad (New Year Yu Sang) 28
    Spring Rolls 12
Char Kway Teow 63
Cha Siew 88
Chicken
    Chicken Marsala Curry 117
    Congee with Chicken (Gai Jook) 43
    Curry Puffs 15
    Hainanese Chicken Rice 57
    Homemade Chicken Stock 167
    Hot and Sour Soup (Suen Laht Tong) 24
    Malaysian Chicken Satay 20
    Malaysian Curry Laksa (Kari Laksa Lemak) 74
    Nonya Curry Chicken 118
    Singapore Noodles 66
    Soya Sauce Chicken (See Yau Gai) 87
    Steamed Chicken with Mushrooms 100
    Stewed Chicken with Mushrooms and Potatoes 101
    Thai Green Curry Chicken 123
Chicken Marsala Curry 117
Chicken Rice, Hainanese 57
Chicken Satay, Malaysian 20
Chicken, Soya Sauce 87
Chicken stock
    Belly Pork with Preserved Vegetable (Mui Choy Kau Yoke) 106
    Congee (Jook) 43
    Hot and Sour Soup (Suen Laht Tong) 24
    Thai Hot and Sour Soup with Prawns (Tom Yum Goong) 30
Chicken Stock, Homemade 167
Chiffon Cake, Jeanie's 157
Chilli
    Beef Rendang 121
    Chilli Paste (for Har Meen) 77
    Chilli Sauce 166
    Garlic & Chilli Sauce 57
    Green Curry Paste 166
    Hot and Sour Fish Laksa (Assam Laksa) 78
    Malaysian Curry Laksa (Kari Laksa Lemak) 74
    Malaysian Pickled Vegetables (Acar Awak) 19
    Nam Jim Sauce 167
    Nonya Curry Chicken 118
    Prawn Sambal 59
    Rempah Paste 167
Chilli Sauce 166
Chinese Almond Cookies 135
Chinese BBQ Pork 88
Chinese Steamed Dumplings 40
Ching Bo Leung 127
Ching Tong Ngau Larm 81
Coconut
    Beef Rendang 121
    Coconut Rice (Nasi Lemak) 58
    Malaysian Curry Laksa (Kari Laksa Lemak) 74
    Mango with Sticky Rice 151
    Nine Layer Kuih (Kow Chan Goh) 132
    Nonya Curry Chicken 118
    Sago Snowballs or Sago Slices 136

Sago with Gula Melaka 144
Seeded Oaty Slice 165
Sweet Potato and Taro in Coconut Milk (Bubur Cha-Cha) 142
Thai Green Curry Chicken 123

Coconut Rice 58
Congee 43
Congee with Chicken 43
Cookies, Chinese Almond 135
Crème Caramel 153
Crispy Pork Belly 91
Cucumber
  Beijing Spicy Sauce Noodles (Zha Jeung Mein) 69
  Hot and Sour Fish Laksa (Assam Laksa) 78
  Malaysian Chicken Satay 20
  Malaysian Pickled Vegetables (Acar Awak) 19
  Prosperity Toss Salad (New Year Yu Sang) 28
Curry
  Beef Rendang 121
  Chicken Marsala Curry 117
  Green Curry Paste 166
  Nonya Curry Chicken 118
  Thai Green Curry Chicken 123
Curry Laksa, Malaysian 74
Curry Puffs 15

D

Daan Taat 130
Daikon
  Beef Broth Noodle Soup (Ching Tong Ngau Larm) 81
  Beef Stew with Daikon and Carrots (Mun Ngau Larm) 105
  Prosperity Toss Salad (New Year Yu Sang) 28
  White Radish Cake (Loh Bak Goh) 46
Dessert
  Almond Jelly with Longan 140
  Chinese Almond Cookies 135
  Crème Caramel 153
  Egg Tarts (Daan Taat) 130
  Hazelnut Apple Cake with Lemon Icing 160
  Jeanie's Chiffon Cake 157
  Jeanie's Mango Pudding 138

Mango with Sticky Rice 151
  Nine Layer Kuih (Kow Chan Goh) 132
  Pavlova 154
  Pineapple and Apple Slice 163
  Sago Snowballs or Sago Slices 136
  Sago with Gula Melaka 144
Dessert soup
  Green Papaya and Longan Dessert Soup 146
  Sweet Potato and Taro in Coconut Milk (Bubur Cha-Cha) 142
  Sweet Red Bean Soup (Hung Dau Saa) 149
Dumplings
  Chinese Steamed Dumplings (Siu Mai) 40
  Pan Fried Pork Dumplings (War Tip) 16
  Short Soup Dumplings (Wonton) 45
Dumpling Sauce 16

E

Egg
  Braised Beef Shin with Soya Eggs (Hung Siu Ngau Yook) 85
  Braised Belly Pork Ribs with Eggs 103
  Crème Caramel 153
  Egg Tarts (Daan Taat) 130
  Fried Rice with Prawns and Larp Cheong 55
  Jeanie's Chiffon Cake 157
  Pavlova 154
  Prawn Noodle Soup (Har Meen) 77
  Steamed Silken Egg with Pork Mince (Jee Yook Jing Daan) 94
Egg Noodles with Oyster Sauce, Tossed 44
Egg Tarts 130

F

Fish
  Hot and Sour Fish Laksa (Assam Laksa) 78
  Prosperity Toss Salad (New Year Yu Sang) 28
  Steamed Whole Fish with Ginger and Shallots 109
  Thai Fish Cakes 23

Tofu and Vegetables Stuffed with Fish Paste (Yong Tau Foo) 110
Fish Cakes, Thai 23
Five Spice Powder 166
Fried fish cake
  Hawker Style Fried Noodles (Mee Goreng) 65
  Malaysian Curry Laksa (Kari Laksa Lemak) 74
  Prawn Noodle Soup (Har Meen) 77
  Stir Fried Flat Rice Noodles (Char Kway Teow) 63
Fried Kang Kong Belachan 51
Fried Rice with Prawns and Larp Cheong 55
Fried Shallots 166

G

Gai Jook 43
Grandma's Tofu 99
Green Curry Chicken, Thai 123
Green Curry Paste 166
Green Papaya and Longan Dessert Soup 146
Green Papaya Salad 36

H

Hainanese Chicken Rice 57
Har Meen 77
Hawker Style Fried Noodles 65
Hazelnut Apple Cake with Lemon Icing 160
Herbal Soup, Nourishing 127
Hokkien noodles see Noodles
Homemade Chicken Stock 167
Hot and Sour Fish Laksa 78
Hot and Sour Soup 24
Hot and Sour Soup with Prawns, Thai 30
Hung Dau Saa 149
Hung Siu Ngau Yook 85

I

Ikan Bilis 59
Ikan Bilis Sambal 59

J

Jai, New Year 114

Jap Chae 73
Jeanie's Chiffon Cake 157
Jeanie's Mango Pudding 138
Jee Par Farn 60
Jee Yook Jing Daan 94
Jing Yook Beng 96
Jook 43

K

Kang Kong Belachan, Fried 51
Kari Laksa Lemak 74
Korean Sweet Potato Noodles 73
Kow Chan Goh 132
Kuih, Nine Layer 132
Kumara *see* Sweet potato

L

Laksa, Assam 78
Laksa, Malaysian Curry 74
Larb Woon Sen 32
Larp cheong
    Fried Rice with Prawns and Larp Cheong 55
    Sang Choy Bao 27
    Stir Fried Flat Rice Noodles (Char Kway Teow) 55
    Taro Cake (Woo Tau Goh) 49
    White Radish Cake (Loh Bak Goh) 46
Lemon Icing 160
Lettuce
    Hot and Sour Fish Laksa (Assam Laksa) 78
    Prosperity Toss Salad (New Year Yu Sang) 28
    Sang Choy Bao 27
    Thai Beef Salad 35
Loh Bak Goh 46
Lo Mein 44

M

Malaysian Chicken Satay 20
Malaysian Curry Laksa 74
Malaysian Pickled Vegetables 19
Mango Pudding, Jeanie's 138
Mango with Sticky Rice 151
Mapo Tofu 99
Master Sauce (soy) 87
Mee Goreng 65

Mui Choy Kau Yoke 106
Mun Ngau Larm 105
Mushrooms
    Beijing Spicy Sauce Noodles (Zha Jeung Mein) 69
    Braised Tofu with Shiitake Mushrooms 112
    Buddha's Delight (New Year Jai) 114
    Chinese Steamed Dumplings (Siu Mai) 40
    Hot and Sour Soup (Suen Laht Tong) 24
    Korean Sweet Potato Noodles (Jap Chae) 73
    Steamed Chicken with Mushrooms 100
    Steamed Pork Rissole with Water Chestnuts (Jing Yook Beng) 96
    Stewed Chicken with Mushrooms and Potatoes 101
    Thai Hot and Sour Soup with Prawns (Tom Yum Goong) 30
    Winter Melon Soup (Tung Kwa Tong) 125

N

Nam Jim Sauce 167
Nasi Lemak 58
New Year Jai 114
New Year Yu Sang 28
Nine Layer Kuih 132
Nonya Curry Chicken 118
Noodle soup
    Beef Broth Noodle Soup (Ching Tong Ngau Larm) 81
    Hot and Sour Fish Laksa (Assam Laksa) 78
    Malaysian Curry Laksa (Kari Laksa Lemak) 74
    Prawn Noodle Soup (Har Meen) 77
Noodles
    Beijing Spicy Sauce Noodles (Zha Jeung Mein) 69
    Hawker Style Fried Noodles (Mee Goreng) 65
    Korean Sweet Potato Noodles (Jap Chae) 73
    Pad Thai 70
    Singapore Noodles 66
    Stir Fried Flat Rice Noodles (Char Kway Teow) 63
    Thai Spicy Pork Bean Thread Noodle Salad (Larb Woon Sen) 32
    Tossed Egg Noodles in Oyster Sauce (Lo Mein) 44
Nourishing Herbal Soup 127

O

Oat
    Seeded Oaty Slice 165

P

Pad Thai 70
Pan Fried Pork Dumplings 16
Pavlova 154
Peanuts
    Dried Anchovies (Ikan Bilis) 59
    Green Papaya Salad (Som Tum) 36
    Ikan Bilis Sambal 59
    Malaysian Pickled Vegetables (Acar Awak) 19
    Pad Thai 70
    Satay Sauce 20
Peanut Sauce *see* Satay Sauce
Peanuts, Roasted 167
Pineapple and Apple Slice 163
Pork
    Beijing Spicy Sauce Noodles (Zha Jeung Mein) 69
    Belly Pork with Preserved Vegetable (Mui Choy Kau Yoke) 106
    Braised Belly Pork Ribs with Eggs 103
    Chinese Steamed Dumplings (Siu Mai) 40
    Chinese BBQ Pork (Cha Siew) 88
    Crispy Pork Belly (Siu Yook) 91
    Korean Sweet Potato Noodles (Jap Chae) 73
    Nourishing Herbal Soup (Ching Bo Leung) 127
    Pan Fried Pork Dumplings (War Tip) 16
    Pork Chop Rice (Jee Par Farn) 60
    Prawn Noodle Soup (Har Meen) 77
    Sang Choy Bao 27
    Short Soup Dumplings (Wonton) 45
    Spring Rolls 12

Steamed Pork Rissole with Water
   Chestnuts (Jing Yook Beng) 96
Steamed Silken Egg with Pork Mince (Jee
   Yook Jing Daan) 94
Thai Spicy Pork Bean Thread Noodle
   Salad (Larb Woon Sen) 32
Winter Melon Soup
   (Tung Kwa Tong) 125

Pork Chop Rice 60

Potato
   Chicken Marsala Curry 117
   Curry Puffs 15
   Hawker Style Fried Noodles
      (Mee Goreng) 65
   Nonya Curry Chicken 118
   Stewed Chicken with Mushrooms and
      Potatoes 101

Prawn Noodle Soup 77

Prawn Sambal 59

Prawns
   Chinese Steamed Dumplings
      (Siu Mai) 40
   Fried Rice with Prawns and Larp
      Cheong 55
   Green Papaya Salad (Som Tum) 36
   Malaysian Curry Laksa
      (Kari Laksa Lemak) 74
   Pad Thai 70
   Prawn Noodle Soup (Har Meen) 77
   Prawn Sambal 59
   Singapore Noodles 66
   Steamed Tofu with Prawn Paste 92
   Stir Fried Flat Rice Noodles
      (Char Kway Teow) 63
   Thai Hot and Sour Soup with Prawns
      (Tom Yum Goong) 30
   Winter Melon Soup
      (Tung Kwa Tong) 125

Prosperity Toss Salad 28

R

Radish Cake, White 46
Red Bean Soup, Sweet 149
Rempah Paste 167
Rice
   Coconut Rice (Nasi Lemak) 58
   Congee (Jook) 43
   Congee with Chicken (Gai Jook) 43
   Fried Rice with Prawns and Larp
      Cheong 55

Hainanese Chicken Rice 57
Mango with Sticky Rice 151
Pork Chop Rice (Jee Par Farn) 60

Rice flour
   Nine Layer Kuih (Kow Chan Goh) 132
   Taro Cake (Woo Tau Goh) 49
   White Radish Cake (Loh Bak Goh) 46

Rice noodles *see* Noodles
Rice Porridge *see* Congee
Roasted Peanuts 167

S

Sago
   Sago Snowballs or Sago Slices 136
   Sago with Gula Melaka 144
   Sweet Potato and Taro in Coconut Milk
      (Burbur Cha-Cha) 142

Sago Slices 136
Sago Snowballs 136
Sago with Gula Melaka 144

Salad
   Green Papaya Salad (Som Tum) 36
   Prosperity Toss Salad
      (New Year Yu Sang) 28
   Thai Beef Salad 35
   Thai Spicy Pork Bean Thread Noodle
      Salad (Larb Woon Sen) 32

Sambal, Ikan Bilis 59
Sambal, Prawn 59
Sang Choy Bao 27
Satay, Malaysian Chicken 20
Satay Sauce 20

Sauce
   Chilli Sauce 166
   Dumpling Sauce 16
   Garlic & Chilli Sauce 57
   Master Sauce (soy) 87
   Nam Jim Sauce 167
   Satay Sauce 20
   Shallot & Ginger Sauce 57
   Sweet & Sour Sauce 12

Seeded Oaty Slice 165
See Yau Gai 87
Shallots, Fried 166
Short Soup Dumplings 45

Shrimps, dried
   Fried Kang Kong Belachan 51

Malaysian Curry Laksa
   (Kari Laksa Lemak) 74
Pad Thai 70
Prawn Noodle Soup (Har Meen) 77
Snake Beans with Dried Shrimps 50
Taro Cake (Woo Tau Goh) 49
Thai Spicy Pork Bean Thread Noodle
   Salad (Larb Woon Sen) 32
White Radish Cake (Loh Bak Goh) 46

Singapore Noodles 66
Siu Mai 40
Siu Yook 91
Slices
   Nine Layer Kuih (Kow Chan Goh) 132
   Pineapple and Apple Slice 163
   Sago Slices 136
   Seeded Oaty Slice 165

Snake Beans with Dried Shrimps 50
Som Tum 36
Soup
   Beef Broth Noodle Soup
      (Ching Tong Ngau Larm) 81
   Hot and Sour Fish Laksa
      (Assam Laksa) 78
   Hot and Sour Soup
      (Suen Laht Tong) 24
   Malaysian Curry Laksa
      (Kari Laksa Lemak) 74
   Nourishing Herbal Soup
      (Ching Bo Leung) 127
   Prawn Noodle Soup (Har Meen) 77
   Thai Hot and Sour Soup with Prawns
      (Tom Yum Goong) 30
   Winter Melon Soup
      (Tung Kwa Tong) 125

Soup, sweet
   Green Papaya and Longan Dessert Soup
      146
   Nourishing Herbal Soup
      (Ching Bo Leung) 127
   Sweet Potato and Taro in Coconut Milk
      (Bubur Cha-Cha) 142
   Sweet Red Bean Soup
      (Hung Dau Saa) 149

Soya Eggs 85
Soya Sauce Chicken 87
Spring Rolls 12

Squid
    Hawker Style Fried Noodles (Mee Goreng) 65
Steamed cake
    Nine Layer Kuih (Kow Chan Goh) 132
    Taro Cake (Woo Tau Goh) 49
    White Radish Cake (Loh Bak Goh) 46
Steamed Chicken with Mushrooms 100
Steamed Dumplings, Chinese 40
Steamed Pork Rissole with Water Chestnuts 96
Steamed Silken Egg with Pork Mince 94
Steamed Tofu with Prawn Paste 92
Steamed Whole Fish with Ginger and Shallots 109
Stewed Chicken with Mushrooms and Potatoes 101
Sticky Rice, Mango with 151
Stir Fried Flat Rice Noodles (Char Kway Teow) 63
Stock, Homemade Chicken 167
Suen Laht Tong 24
Sweet & Sour Sauce 12
Sweet Potato and Taro in Coconut Milk 142
Sweet Potato Noodles, Korean 73
Sweet Red Bean Soup 149

T

Tapico *see* Sago
Taro
    Sweet Potato and Taro in Coconut Milk (Bubur Cha-Cha) 142
    Taro Cake (Woo Tau Goh) 49
Taro Cake 49
Thai Beef Salad 35
Thai Fish Cakes 23
Thai Green Curry Chicken 123
Thai Hot and Sour Soup with Prawns 30
Thai Spicy Pork Bean Thread Noodle Salad 32
Toasted Belachan 167
Tofu
    Braised Tofu with Shiitake Mushrooms 112
    Buddha's Delight (New Year Jai) 114

`Hawker Style Fried Noodles (Mee Goreng) 65
Hot and Sour Soup (Suen Laht Tong) 24
Malaysian Curry Laksa (Kari Laksa Lemak) 74
Pad Thai 70
Steamed Tofu with Prawn Paste 92
Tofu and Vegetables Stuffed with Fish Paste (Yong Tau Foo) 110
Tofu and Vegetables Stuffed with Fish Paste 110
Tom Yum Goong 30
Tung Kwa Tong 125

V

Vegetables
    Fried Kang Kong Belachan 51
    Malaysian Pickled Vegetables (Acar Awak) 19
    Snake Beans with Dried Shrimps 50
    Tofu and Vegetables Stuffed with Fish Paste (Yong Tau Foo) 110
Vegetarian
    Almond Jelly with Longan 140
    Braised Tofu with Shiitake Mushrooms 112
    Buddha's Delight (New Year Jai) 114
    Chinese Almond Cookies 135
    Crème Caramel 153
    Egg Tarts (Daan Taat) 130
    Green Papaya Salad (Som Tum) 36
    Hazelnut Apple Cake with Lemon Icing 160
    Jeanie's Chiffon Cake 157
    Korean Sweet Potato Noodles (Jap Chae) 73
    Malaysian Pickled Vegetables (Acar Awak) 19
    Mango with Sticky Rice 151
    Nourishing Herbal Soup (Ching Bo Leung) 127
    Pavlova 154
    Pineapple and Apple Slice 163
    Sago Snowballs or Sago Slices 136
    Sago with Gula Melaka 144
    Seeded Oaty Slice 165

Sweet Potato and Taro in Coconut Milk (Bubur Cha-Cha) 142
Sweet Red Bean Soup (Hung Dau Saa) 149

W

Water chestnuts
    Sang Choy Bao 27
    Spring Rolls 12
    Steamed Pork Rissole with Water Chestnuts (Jing Yook Beng) 96
White radish *see* Daikon
White Radish Cake 46
Winter Melon Soup 125
Wonton 45
Woo Tau Goh 49

Y

Yam *see* Taro
Yellow noodles *see* Noodles
Yong Tau Foo 110
Yu Sang 28

Z

Zha Jeung Mein 69

Jeanie Lau was born in Ipoh, Malaysia. When she was young, her family ran an imported foods specialty store and wholesale outlet. Her father would import exotic food products and the best and freshest fruits from all over the world. Her love of food started at a young age when her father would take the family everywhere to eat, so they could try all sorts of cuisines from many different cultures.

She emigrated to Australia when she was 19, to study in a business college. The rest of her family emigrated to Australia in 1972. She worked in the Sydney Stock Exchange before travelling overseas. When she returned to Sydney, she took up a role in an insurance company. It was then that she met Eddie, who was living in Canberra and working as a clerk in the Commonwealth Public Service at the time. After marrying Eddie, she moved to Canberra, where she worked for the Australian Bureau of Statistics.

In Canberra, "pot luck" dinners with friends and neighbours were a frequent affair. Over the years, Jeanie has developed quite a reputation for her cooking and baking, with friends and family often requesting recipes. She loves to cook for others, and even held a weekly cooking class for her work colleagues for a short time. Her two children, Colin and Katrina, were born in Canberra and she took a break from work to raise them.

In 1985, Eddie left the public service and the family moved to Sydney. Eddie was then involved with the family food business and later decided to go into the cafe business. Jeanie's family, her brother Bernard, sister Jenny, brother-in-law and nephew, have owned and run a number of food outlets, restaurants and cafes in Sydney for over 40 years. Her father-in-law had a Chinese takeaway since the 1960s. Once reunited in Sydney, big family dinners became a weekly event where 10–12 of them would all come together to share food around one large table.

More recently, she became a grandparent and retired from working in the food industry (though she's still been known to start baking at 4am in the morning). When she recently turned 70, her family thought the best gift for her would be to document all her treasured recipes. They did this by creating a cookbook full of memories and good food, to pass down the generations, especially to her grandchildren.

Katrina Lau Hammond was born in Canberra, Australia, into a family of food lovers. As a child, she often played near the family restaurant in Sydney, and sometimes, even served customers. Her mother showed her how to bake and cook when she was a child, giving her a confidence in the kitchen at an early age. Her fascination with food continued into high school and later university, where she studied food science and marketing at UNSW, including a year at the agricultural college UC Davis.

She worked in the corporate world for a number of years as a food technologist in quality assurance, product development, and food safety; as well as in sales and in marketing, but always in the food industry. When the creativity and travel bugs wouldn't stop biting her, she quit the corporate food world to return to school. But this time in a French cooking school in Paris, to learn to become a pâtissière and boulangère. She worked as a pastry chef and baker in Paris, London and the Netherlands, before returning to Sydney with her husband to have their first child. She then worked part-time in her own business as a food technologist, pastry chef and food photographer.

Her second child was born shortly after and since then, she has run the cancer gauntlet non-stop for almost 5 years. In that time, she has occasional creative sparks, like the idea that turned into this project. And another that resulted in a children's picture book about cancer, called *The Village*, to be released in August 2021. She is currently living with metastatic breast cancer and receiving ongoing cancer treatment, but is determined to see her mum's book completed and being shared among family and friends.

Katrina's 3rd birthday butterfly cake

Jeanie's Cooking Class with work collegues, Canberra 1980's.

Jeanie, Eddie, Mackenzie at Yum cha 2017

Colin's 2nd birthday party train cake

Lau family on Boxing Day 2004

Making fresh pasta together, 2018

Colin's 4th birthday party, humpty dumpty cake

Preparing suckling pig stuffing for christmas lunch 2015

Katrina's 1st birthday party bunny cake

Danny, Eddie, Colin's 2nd birthday car cake

Family trip to Japan, Osaka 2019

Colin, Jeanie, Katrina after after moving to Sydney 1985

Crab catch & feast at Col & Mei's place with Bianca, Derek, Bernard Xmas 2020

Katrina feeding Colin jelly, Canberra 1983

Jeanie and Colin trying jook and vegemite toast, 1979

Making desserts with their grandchildren, 2020

Sampling seafood at Tsukiji fish markets, Japan 2019

Jeanie and her siblings with their mother, Regal Restaurant, Sydney 1996

Jeanie's birthday 1981

Mackenzie's 5th birthday afternoon tea party

Jeanie and Eddie 1974

Justin's big catch, Lake Macquarie 2020

Jeanie, Bernard, Katrina, Eddie, Mackenzie, Chinese New Year 2021

Jeanie adding the final touches to Yu Sang dish for YanYet 2021

John, Jody, Colin celebrating Justin's birthday 2019

Jeanie preparing the boys' catch of the day 2020

Feast for Jeanie's 50th surprise birthday party 2000

Lunch for Jeanie's 70th

Sisters Jeanie, Jenny & Sue 1970's

Eddie's 74th birthday

www.ingramcontent.com/pod-product-compliance
Lightning Source LLC
Chambersburg PA
CBHW042350300426
44109CB00038B/120